## Testimonials

*"Warwick John Fahy is an incredible communicator. This book proves it! Every business presenter should not just read it, but internalize it!"*
Darren LaCroix, 2001 World Champion of Public Speaking.

*"Great leaders are great communicators. Shorten your time to the top with one of the best resources on the market for bettering your speaking skills. It's a must for anyone who wants to effectively convey their ideas."*
Scott Friedman, Past President, National Speakers Association.

*"A must-read for anyone whose livelihood depends on communicating through effective presentations."*
Subramu Basavapatna, Project Manager, Siemens PLM.

*"The difference between the right book about business presentations and others is the difference between lightning and the lightning bug. This book is the lightning. This is the landmark book on business presentations."*
Michael Michalko, author, *Thinkertoys* (A Handbook of Creative Thinking Techniques).

*"An essential resource for every business presenter. Keep it on your desk or in your briefcase."*
Harry E. Chambers, author, *My Way or the Highway: The Micromanagement Survival Guide.*

*"Powerful, perceptive and practical advice for anyone presenting in a world of shortening attention spans. Use this book and profit."*
Suzanne Bates, President and CEO Bates Communications Inc., author, *Speak Like a CEO* and *Motivate Like a CEO.*

*"Warwick John Fahy has filled this book with practical tips to help you communicate effectively, which is one of the most important keys to business success today."*
Jim Key, 2003 World Champion of Public Speaking.

*"In The One Minute Presenter, Warwick John Fahy helps you overcome some of the biggest obstacles people face on their way to top. Buy it - read it - profit from it."*

W Mitchell, CPAE, 2008-2009 President of the International Federation of Professional Speakers.

*"Your level of success will depend upon your level of communication through effective presentation skills. Warwick's book, The One Minute Presenter, provides you with the disciplines which will make that difference to your the bottom line!"*

Bob Urichuck, International Professional Speaker, trainer and Author, *Discipline for Life, You Are the Author of Your Future.*

*"Who better than a master practitioner to deliver this brilliant message brilliantly? Five stars."*

Rodney Marks, Past President, National Speakers Association of Australia.

*"Here is a helpful and easy-to-read resource that is loaded with insights on presenting to people with low attention spans. It's loaded with intelligent tips and techniques you can start to use and benefit from immediately."*

Robyn Pearce the Time Queen, Certified Speaking Professional, Past President, IFFPS (International Federation for Professional Speakers).

*"The One-Minute Presenter is overflowing with speaking tips, is absolutely fascinating and lots of fun. In eight easy steps, Fahy shows you how to perform like a pro."*

Dan Poynter, author, *The Self-Publishing Manual.*

*"Valuable research on why presenters often fail to make the impact they want. Practical and innovative success steps with immediate and long term benefits."*

Raleigh R. Pinskey, The Raleigh Group Communications, author, *101 Ways To Promote Yourself, The 8-Second Media Pitch* and *Branding Basics.*

*"I rate this book unquestionably a "must" for anyone that is required to do presentations. From big audiences to the small negotiation table, the principles and practical techniques hold true for both. Warwick has been able to capture the true essence of what it means to successfully present and get great outcomes. He writes not just for the intellectual mind but to the heart also."*

Allison Mooney, professional speaker and author, New Zealand Speaker of the Year 05/06, Most Inspirational Speaker of the Year 07.

*"Self belief is essential for peak performance. A lack of confidence in public speaking holds back many business executives. This book is packed with techniques to take your next business presentation to a higher level."*

John Shackleton CSP, The Performance Expert.


*"Practical, full of excellent content, quick and easy to digest! A must buy for anyone in the business of speaking and presenting."*

Matthias Gelber, Winner, Greenest Person on the Planet 2008


*"Warwick has produced this helpful and easy-to-read resource that is loaded with insights on presenting to a variety of audiences. It's loaded with intelligent tips and techniques you can start to use and benefit from immediately."*

Mark Millar, Vice President, Supply Chain Asia. Founding Member, Professional Speakers Association of China.


*"Presentations are my life. Every day I'm 'moving' audiences to new levels of understanding and inspiration. If you'd like to do that – look no further than this great guide. Warwick John Fahy is renowned for his ability to move and inspire and to do that in one of the most challenging markets in the world. You'll be so grateful he's captured EVERYTHING (as in every thing) you need right here in these pages."*

Paul Dunn, entrepreneur, marketeer and speaker, Co-Founder of Buy1GIVE1


*"The code for successful business presentations has been broken and the secrets for success are here in this book! If you are a business executive or professional, and want to present with confidence, buy this book."*

Donna Hickey MBA, international professional speaker


*"Never bore your audience again! Learn and apply the techniques in this book and you will deliver more engaging presentations with less preparation time than ever before. I can't wait for the next speech contest."*

Kiminari Azuma, manager, Information Systems, Tyco Electronics. 2007 & 2008, Champion Toastmasters District 76 (Japan), International Speech Contest.


*"Read Warwick's unique approach on how to reach a new generation of speakers with these effective tips on how to improve your presentations skills."*

Keith E Ostergard, president & chief Consultant, LPC Consulting

# The One Minute Presenter

8 steps to successful business presentations
in a short attention span world

## Warwick John Fahy

**Unique Voices Publishing**

Original Edition
Hong Kong
2009

Published by Unique Voices Publishing Limited
Level 39
One Exchange Square
8 Connaught Place
Central, Hong Kong

Cover Author Photo: *Delphy Chow*
Interior Design: *Kathrin Zimmermann*
Author Coach: *Lorna McLeod*
Author Mentor: *John Robert Eggen*
Illustrator: *Marini Widowati*

Copyright 2009 by Warwick John Fahy
First Edition, January 2009
ISBN 978-988-1805

*This book is available at special quantity discounts to use as premiums and sales
promotions, or for use in corporate training programs. For more information, please
email premium@oneminutepresenter.com*

This book is dedicated to Mum.

"You're the best!"

"The mark of a good action is that it appears inevitable in retrospect."

*Robert Louis Stevenson, Scottish novelist,*
*author, Treasure Island, 1850-1894.*

## Warning – Disclaimer

This book is designed to provide information on how to become a more effective presenter. It's sold with the understanding that the publisher and the author are not engaged in rendering legal, accounting or other professional services. If legal or other expert assistance is required, the services of a competent professional should be sought.

It's not the purpose of this book to reprint all the information that is otherwise available to authors and/or publishers, but instead to complement, amplify and supplement other texts. You are urged to read all the available material, learn as much as possible about presentations and tailor the information to your individual needs.

Every effort has been made to make this book as complete and as accurate as possible. However, there may be mistakes, both typographical and in content. Therefore, this text should be used only as a general guide and not as the ultimate source of presenting information. Furthermore, this book contains information on presenting that is current only up to the printing date.

The purpose of this book is to educate and entertain. The author and the publisher shall have neither liability nor responsibility to any person or entity with respect to any loss or damage caused, or alleged to have been caused, directly or indirectly, by the information contained in this book.

**If you do not wish to be bound by the above, you may return this book to the publisher for a full refund.**

# Contents

# About the Author

Warwick is Asia's leading business presentation coach working with senior executives, business leaders and entrepreneurs who need to influence clients, investors, shareholders and team members. His down-to-earth practical approach and deep cross cultural understanding have made him a sought after business presentation coach throughout Asia.

## Public speaking pioneer

Warwick was inducted into the Hall of Fame in 2007 by Toastmasters International, the world's largest public speaking organisation, for his pioneering leadership as chairman in China. He is founding President of the Professional Speakers Association of China and a member of the New York National Speakers Association.

## Business results facilitator

Warwick is invited by multinationals to consult, train and coach executives in the key skills of communication and leadership. Warwick demonstrates deep cultural intelligence while collaborating with teams across China, Asia and the Middle East. He has lived in Asia since 1994 and facilitates in both English and Mandarin. He is an International Association of Facilitators' Certified Professional Facilitator (CPF), granted after demonstrating evidence of competency in five core facilitation areas.

## Enlightened business leader

Warwick serves as general manager of TEAMSWORK China, an accredited social enterprise, which helps retain and develop talent for multinationals through consulting, training and executive coaching services across Asia Pacific and the Middle East. Warwick has been recognised as an enlightened business owner with two nominations for the Extraordinary Life Awards for social entrepreneurs. He has served as an elected committee member for the British Chamber of Commerce in Shanghai. Warwick loves nature and sports, competing in Ironman triathlons.

*More about Warwick is available at www.oneminutepresenter.com.*

# Part I

# – 1 –

# Nobody is Listening

"There's an 800 pound watermelon in the room. And it's your presentation!"

*Warwick John Fahy, author, The One Minute Presenter*

## This chapter's content:

▶ A. Nobody is listening: big red watermelons.
*Page 3*

▶ B. Falling attention spans.
*Page 3*

▶ C. Reasons for information overload.
*Page 7*

▶ D. Multitasking is not good.
*Page 8*

## One Minute learning:

● Your audience doesn't have an unlimited amount of time, attention or energy
*Page 3*

● Nobody is listening because attention spans are falling
*Page 3*

● Technology helps us multitask more. That's not all good
*Page 8*

● People are so crazy busy they act like they have attention deficit disorder (ADD)
*Page 8*

● You need to adjust your presentation style
*Page 9*

## Process:

☞ First, understand why people's attention spans are falling.

☞ Second, realize our modern-day preference for multi-tasking is contributing to our even shorter attention spans.

☞ Third, be clear when someone has a piece of technology in their hands, they are not paying much attention to you.

# A. Nobody is Listening

Imagine a group of people sitting up straight in their seats. Everyone is listening to you. You could hear a pin drop. They are listening very carefully. Their full attention is on your every word. You feel honored to have such a captivated group, who care so much about your knowledge, expertise and experience that they are willing to drop everything and listen.

**Get real, right?**

Do you like watermelon? You know the kind that are piled up in markets, the big green ones with bright red watery flesh inside! Imagine these watermelons are like a person's complete attention span. Take one of these ripe melons. Bring it to the top of a skyscraper building and then drop it (better do this when nobody else is around- those melons can be heavy). The resulting crush of melon on the pavement below is the average person's attention span today: a mess. It's fragmented. It's in bits. People are just not able to focus like they could before. The picture above of a group full of attentive listeners sitting and doting on your every word is a lovely dream, but that's about it. Unless you're using some or all of the techniques in this book, then you're presenting to a room full of crushed watermelons (horrible image, isn't it?). A room full of people who cannot pay attention.

# B. Falling Attention Spans

An **attention span** is the amount of time a person can concentrate on a single activity. It's important when you want to achieve goals, absorb knowledge or hit targets in an archery competition. The great media philosopher and writer, Marshall McLuhan, famous for coining the phrase "the medium is the message", said the average attention span for a TV viewer was four to five minutes. In 1976. Today's action movies are made with cuts every three seconds. So why have people's attention spans been falling so much?

If you're a "digital immigrant" like me, then you have probably become proficient with computers the hard way. Two finger typing, looking for the user manual for your ipod and generally avoiding video games of all kinds.

But surely my initial uses of computers will make you feel better. While taking a compulsory data processing course at university, I went to the computer lab to check my paper results, which were returned on a floppy disk. I popped the disk in, thought for a moment, and then typed the only computer command I could remember, "format disk". I erased all the data from the disk! Now in my defense, this was before Windows, user interfaces and mouses were used.

Feeling better about being a digital immigrant now?

# Technology contributes to low attention spans

Marc Prensky, who coined the word "digital natives", observed that the widespread use of digital technology was contributing to low attention spans. Digital natives, born after 1980, have grown up with access to the internet and know how to use technology intuitively. They think and process information differently. This is important to you because if you're a digital immigrant you need to be aware of the fundamentally different approach you need to take to get your message across.

## Differences between digital natives and digital immigrants:

| | Digital Natives | Digital Immigrants |
|---|---|---|
| Thinking speed | Fast, in bursts. | Slowly, step-by-step. |
| Processing ability | Multitasking. Parallel processing. | One thing at a time. Sequentially. Logically. |
| Type of information | Graphics before text. | Text based. |
| Access to information | Random access (hyperlinked). | Linear. |
| Learning | Networked. | Individual. |
| Incentives | Instant gratification. Frequent rewards. | Paying your dues. |
| Attitudes | Work and learning is "play". | Work and learning is "serious". |
| Attention span highest | During interactivity. | When left to think it through. |

# Other causes to low attention spans

## Boring information

- According to Dr. John Medina, a brain researcher, the brain doesn't pay attention to boring things. So relating too much information, with not enough time to connect the dots results in very little digestion.

## Poor interactions

- Most business information exchanges are one way with low participation so we zone out.

- We make quick judgments about people so if we perceive the topic to be of no interest, we switch our attention to something else.

- Cross cultural issues where the listener does not comprehend your message in English since the listener is converting from English to his or her native language.

## New technology

- Mobile devices compete for our attention constantly. We love sending and receiving messages. Our demand for a constant supply of updated information means we are always glancing at our mobiles reducing our concentration on the task at hand.

## Faster speed of information

- The information age bombards us with information, so we digest it very quickly and look for variety at speed.

- TV shows and movies with constantly changing angles.

- Television is replacing books as main source of information. Prensky estimated that in 2001 college graduates already spent four times as much time on watching TV as reading. And twice as much time on video games.

- TV provides non-linear communication appearing as bursts of sound, pictures and text which quickly change. This trains us to focus for short periods on many different points, but reduces our overall attention span.

## Thinking patterns changed by the environment

- Faced by the information and sensory overload of our modern environment, we have evolved to juggle these incoming inputs so we quickly go from one input to another. Our evolution has caused falling attention spans.

- Younger "digital natives" are hard wired to multitask, which by definition reduces attention span.

- We allow our children to grow up in a multitasking multi-stimulus environment. From an early age, our children have so many more things competing for their attention. Doing homework while watching TV, instant messaging on the computer, texting friends by phone, playing tunes on an ipod, and reading textbooks all at the same time!

## Consumer choice

- Too much choice. So we tend to change brands more frequently.

- The general public (and this may not apply to you) prefers trivia over substance. This explains the success of TV shows like Pop Idol (globally), the private life disclosures of pop stars becoming front page news and the continuing idolizing of superficial beauty (advertising).

## Working style

- Push for "increased productivity" at work. We are overworked, stressed out and don't have enough time. This anxiety means we are always thinking about what else we should be doing.

- The knowledge economy requires a different skillset to manufacturing. An information intensive working environment cultivates an aptitude for a low attention span.

- We are so focused on trivial small tasks that we spend the whole day jumping from one small task to another without regard for the big picture.

These all contribute to falling attention spans. But why is that a problem? It's a problem becuase we have to process more information today than ever before.

# C. Reasons for Information Overload

| Reasons for Information Overload | Why we like it |
| --- | --- |
| 24-hour cable TV | Lots of choice:<br>From CNN and BBC 24 for news, MTV for music, HBO for movies. |
| The Internet | Always on:<br>Emails, surfing, researching. |
| Video games | Too much fun:<br>Engaging and fully immersive virtual experiences (wow!). |
| Messaging | We love to stay in touch:<br>Mobile text messages, MSN, G Talk, Twitter. |
| Newspapers | Stay informed:<br>Sunday newspapers with their many supplements have more information than our grandparents read in their whole lives! |
| Magazines | It's about me:<br>Every available niche and special interest catered for. |
| Publishing | We can all be publishers:<br>Blogs, Wikipedia, print on demand. |
| Social networking | To be connected:<br>Myspace, Facebook, YouTube. |

We have too many fun distractions competing for our attention. We are too busy. We need to multitask.

# D. Multitasking is Not Good

Multitasking is when we do more than one thing at the same time. Like this:

| Primary Task | Multitasking |
|---|---|
| Reading a newspaper while... | ...checking mobile device, chatting online. |
| Listening to the TV while... | ...playing with a mobile device, texting, surfing. |
| Writing an email while... | ...quickly checking messages, listening to music. |
| Speaking while... | ...checking BlackBerry, reading messages. |

Multitasking is not good. According to *Brain Rules* author and neuroscientist, Dr. John Medina, the human brain's **attentional spotlight** is incapable of multitasking. The fact that we appear to be able to adapt to simultaneous inputs doesn't actually mean that multitasking is occurring.

## Multitasking doesn't help

Dr. Edward M. Hallowell, psychiatrist and author of *Crazy Busy*, observes that this state of being too busy has created "culturally induced attention deficit disorder." One major factor according to Dr. Hallowell is technology. Our modern skills of balancing our computers, cellphones and BlackBerrys can cause us to look like we have ADD. That doesn't sound like a good thing, does it?

Just talk to someone who is "crazy busy". Most of them love it. In Shanghai *"I'm very busy"* has almost replaced *"Hello, how are you?"* as a greeting. It's fun to play with our mobile toys. We like being connected. We feel important when we can email and surf while sitting in the car or subway. Part of the problem is that gadgets are cool and fun. Even a one-year-old baby can use an iPhone to scroll through photographs. However, the more screen sucking we do, the more mental energy we waste. And this is causing our attention spans to drop like a melon off a skyscraper.

> "When you're always online, you're always distracted."
> *Dr. John Medina*

## So what does this mean for me?

The lesson for you is "Don't present like your audience has an unlimited amount of time, attention or energy." They don't. And if you try to shove a large melon into their mouths, they are going to resist (that's quite a visual). And that's the way most people present: they try to shove large amounts of information at their listeners and are then surprised when the audience switches off mentally, turns to their mobile devices and doesn't get the message.

If you rely on the spoken word to get your job done, then you need to be able to overcome falling attention spans. Because if people aren't listening to you, then you can't be effective. If you're not effective, then you can't be doing your job. This means if you can't adapt to this new way of communication, you will become redundant. The solution is here: this book is designed with busy executives in mind.

It's created to help you prepare for any audience, quickly craft compelling messages, engage and connect with the audience during your presentation and manage every kind of interruption imaginable – including the dreaded Q&A time.

### Next chapter

This book will give you the techniques you need to engage with today's attention deficit listeners. Go get a nice juicy melon, chop it up and read on because "Help is Here".

# – 2 –

# Help is Here

"You get what you give."

*Jack Stack, author, The Great Game of Business.*

**This chapter's content:**

▶ A. Problem: too many presentations.
*Page 13*

▶ B. Solution: a new way of presenting.
*Page 14*

▶ C. Understanding digital natives.
*Page 15*

**One Minute Learning:**

● Information-heavy presentations are easily forgotten
*Page 13*

● Tips to engage your audience
*Page 14*

● Tips for business professionals to be influential
*Page 14*

● Advice field tested by a practitioner
*Page 14*

● Special tips on digital natives
*Page 15*

● Push your comfort zone
*Page 15*

**Process:**

☞ First, think about the last presentation that made you go "Wow!"

☞ Second, skim through the approach this book takes to bring you the most practical approach to influential business presentations.

☞ Third, read about digital natives and how they will change the way you give presentations in the future.

# A. Problem: Too Many Presentations

We learned in Chapter 1 that attention spans are falling due to technology, information overload and multitasking. Added to this, we are bombarded by mind-numbing presentations. Some estimates indicate 30 million presentations are given daily. Have you ever gone "Wow!" during a presentation? Not very often. I have sat through my fair share of boring presentations and probably gave a few of them (a long time ago!). People switch off very quickly, which means if you can't grab their attention and keep them entertained and engaged, your presentation is wasted.

## Your guide

This handbook guides you through the maze of low attention spans. It's designed for busy professionals who need quick and easy access to tips and techniques to engage their frazzled audiences. It's a combination of my own very diverse experiences as an international presenter, coach and facilitator of diverse cultural groups and my research into what it takes to be an awesome presenter in today's information overloaded world. In essence, *The One Minute Presenter*:

- Gets you very focused about your message
- Provides a comprehensive range of quick tips
- Helps you be always ready to present

## PRESENTATIONS TO MAKE YOU GO "WOW!"

Watch Hans Rosling during his "No more boring data" presentation to TED in California in 2006 using the Gapminder tool. Check it out on YouTube. www.youtube.com or www.ted.com.

*See more about Hans a. www.gapminder.org.*

# B. Solution: A New Way of Presenting

Given all these continuing changes, *The One Minute Presenter* helps you avoid obsolescence. Like a good Irish stew, this book has a number of healthy ingredients that contribute to the overall taste.

## Practical tips relevant to business executives

This book includes time tested practical tips which you can use immediately. Growing a million dollar business taught me the lessons of the market as a young sales executive when I was giving 100 presentations a year to technology companies. It's hard to believe now, but at the start of my career, I was thrown out of a presentation by a small trading company owner. Talk about making a connection! I learned the hard way by making this and many more mistakes. Today, I coach senior executives in multinationals to engage with their multicultural teams across Asia and the Middle East. I have used this first -hand knowledge to bring you the best insights into what works for business executives today.

## Advice from a practitioner

I once gave a five-minute speech with 74 "ahhs" in it, but within a year I had won a national public speaking contest. I love public speaking and have spent the last seven years growing the public speaking industry in China as a mentor and leader for Toastmasters International. As both a leader and presenter, I have witnessed thousands of presentations and have compiled the best techniques into this book.

## International best practice

Almost every senior executive today faces a multicultural audience. You need to be able to overcome cultural obstacles and still get your message across in an engaging way. I have traveled across the globe from Asia, the Middle East and America to meet with the best professional speakers and learn from them. I have set up the first professional speaking association in China called the Professional Speakers Association of China to take promising speakers and fast track their careers. The techniques in this book work well across cultures and generations.

## Push your comfort zone

Have you ever heard yourself saying, *"There's no way I would do that!"* Whenever I hear myself saying that, I know there is a learning opportunity around the corner: I have hosted charity auctions, been a stand-up comedian, done improvisational comedy, appeared in Chinese TV variety shows and sitcoms and given hundreds of speeches in English and Mandarin. Follow the eight stations on *The One Minute Presenter's* journey and try them out. They work.

# C. Understanding Digital Natives

### Can you speak digital?

Every person under the age of 25 can speak DSL. DSL means "digital as a second language". According to researchers Ian Jukes and Anita Dosaj, a digital native has learned digital language like a mother tongue. Their findings investigate how people who have grown up in the computer and internet age are hardwired in a different way to receive and interact with information.

In fact, they believe this causes the digital native's brain to be physically different. Advertising guru, Lord Saatchi observes that the digital native's brain *"has rewired itself. It responds faster. It sifts out. It recalls less."*

## HOW CAN I PRESENT TO A DIGITAL NATIVE?

C&T is a theater company with a difference. They place digital technology at the heart of the drama. This has lead them to face the challenges presented by digital natives. According to C&T's producer Rob Lines, one key difference lies in the attitude to receiving information. Digital immigrants watch TV that tells them what happens next, but natives want to participate in the story and affect the outcome. Immigrants love a story with a beginning, middle and end, whilst natives want to custom-assemble their own narrative. Immigrants learn by passively listening – natives learn by actively collaborating.

Throughout this book you can pick up tips that will help you increase the interaction of your presentation and improve your business presentation's effectiveness.

*Learn more about C&T at www.candt.org.*

This explains continuous partial attention (CPA) and why a modern teenager, during a 30-second commercial while watching TV, can:

- Take a telephone call

- Send a text

- Receive a photograph

- Play a game

- Download a music track

- Read a magazine

- Watch commercials at x6 speed

Digital natives are increasingly becoming a part of your customer base and workforce. Today everyone's attention spans are shortening. As a manager and leader you need to be understood, even when you only have a few minutes to express yourself. Pick up tips throughout this book to help you do just that. Your future career could depend on it.

### Next chapter

Next, we'll overview how to best use and learn from this book with "Your Roadmap".

# − 3 −

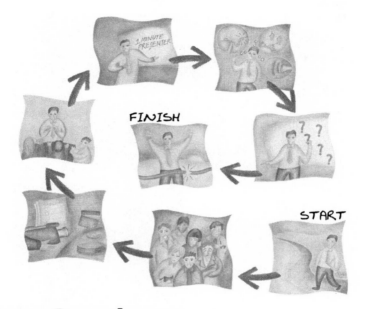

# Your Roadmap

"All you need is the plan, the road map, and the courage to press on to your destination."

*Earl Nightingale, US motivational writer and author, 1921-1989.*

**This chapter's content:**

▶ A. Your Journey.
*Page 19*

▶ B. Three Learning
Speeds.
*Page 20*

**One Minute Learning:**

● Your learning journey
summarized to 34 words
*Page 19*

● Preview the eight stations
on your journey to better
presentations
*Page 19*

● Choose three different
learning tracks
*Page 20*

● Learn from Case studies
*Page 21*

**Process:**

☞ First, scan the road-
map. Tick the chapters/
stations that you need
help with first.

☞ Second, choose a
learning track depen-
ding on how fast you
wish to learn.

☞ Third, dip into this
book before your key
presentations.

# A. Your Journey

*The One Minute Presenter* is a journey. Here's the roadmap. You can choose how to take the journey, which can be boiled down to 34 words:

*"You, the presenter must treasure your audience to produce your message. Once you create your connection, you can deliver with style {with technology}, manage all interruptions, master the Q&A to finish on time."*

**The 8 stations are:**

**1** — **You, the Presenter**
See page 25

**2** — **Treasure your Audience**
See page 41

**3** — **Produce your Message**
See page 55

**4** — **Create your Connection**
See page 73

**5** — **Deliver with Style (with technology)**
See page 93

**6** — **Manage all Interruptions**
See page 133

**7** — **Master the Q&A**
See page 153

**8** — **Finish on Time**
See page 169

# B. Three Learning Speeds

**You can read this book at three different speeds:**

- **Step by Step**
  Start from Chapter 4 and work through.

- **Jump Around**
  Focus on areas you need help with now.

- **Jet Ski**
  Skim each chapter's first page to catch the One Minute Learning points.

## Step by Step

There are 8 stations along the journey. Read through each chapter in detail. Look at the sidebars. Make notes, underline and highlight words. Take your time at the stations which are new to you or where you need more help. Visit **www.oneminutepresenter.com** for the latest tips.

## Jump Around

### Case study

Read case studies at the beginning of each chapter. Each case study is based on real life situations faced by business professionals like you every day. If you resonate with the issues in the case study, spend more time on the chapter. Tips are provided throughout each chapter to the problems faced in the case. Here is the list of all the case studies:

**Case study#1:** Roger, IT general manager, manufacturing.
*See page 27*

**Case study#2:** Mike, marketing manager, consumer goods.
*See page 43*

**Case study#3:** Dave, sales engineer, software industry.
*See page 57*

**Case study#4:** Paul, country manager, specialty chemicals.
*See page 75*

**Case study#5:** J.S. Chen, finance director, semiconductors.
*See page 95*

**Case study#6:** Enmo Noma, chairman, industrial services.
*See page 135*

**Case study#7:** Ann, human resources director, professional services.
*See page 155*

**Case study#8:** Tim, technical director, mobile technology.
*See page 171*

## Sidebars

Sidebars provide extra information related to the topic. Every chapter has sidebars which deepens the learning for the chapter's topic.

## Resources

Resources section at the back of the book on page 187 contains web links for every chapter so you can explore more expert advice. You can also see the updated resources links online at **www.oneminutepresenter.com/resources.**

## Jet Ski

You can overview the whole journey by turning to the first page of every chapter and reading the chapter content and One Minute Learning in bullet points. Next to each One Minute Learning, you can find a page number, which will take you directly to this tip. Read also the ***Process,*** which, like a cooking recipe, will give you the steps to complete each chapter. You can also download a PDF version "cheat sheet" for each chapter's key learning at

**www.oneminutepresenter.com/keylearnings**

## Next chapter

Next, we start with your journey: "You, the Presenter", where you will learn how to get yourself ready and overcome any fear you have about speaking to a group.

# Part II

# – 4 –

# You, the Presenter

"You gain strength, courage and confidence by every experience in which you really stop to look fear in the face. You must do the thing you think you cannot do."

*Eleanor Roosevelt, US diplomat & reformer, 1884 – 1962.*

## This chapter's content:

## One Minute Learning:

## *Process:*

☞ First, check your current speaking strengths.

☞ Second, view a quick checklist on becoming a more authentic speaker.

☞ Third, overcome fear with six powerful strategies.

# Case study#1:
## *Roger, IT general manager, manufacturing.*

Roger was a successful executive working with an international technology company. Having just completed his MBA, he was promoted to general manager. In his new role, he would have to give more public presentations to his team in China and the head office in California.

Despite a strong technical background and good industry knowledge, Roger was never comfortable before an important presentation. Up to a week before, a general feeling of anxiety came over him which stopped him from sleeping well at night. On the day, and even hours before, he felt sick while his hands were cold and sweaty. As he stepped up to present, his mouth went dry and his heart was pounding. He could feel his throat tighten and his knees felt weak. He took a few rapid breaths and with trembling lips took his first words.

Maybe you can relate. Have you ever felt nervous before a public presentation? Do you know why? This chapter looks at the causes and solutions.

# A. Rate Yourself

This chapter is all about "being you", and all the things which go through your mind (and body) before you get anywhere near an audience. Start by rating yourself with *The One Minute Questionnaire*.

Take this assessment to understand your current strengths and areas to improve. The following chapters of this book (chapters 4 to 11) give you practical tips to help build up your *One Minute Presenter* abilities:

## The One Minute Questionnaire

As you complete this self assessment, notice that each heading in the questionnaire corresponds to one of the 8 stations of the *One Minute Presenter* journey.

**Answer each statement with a:**

Y      "Yes"

N      "No"

NS     "Not Sure"

**You, the Presenter**

_____You are a master in all aspects of presenting

_____You are completely calm before presenting

_____You have found your voice as a presenter

**Treasure your Audience**

_____You understand what motivates your audience

_____You have a profile of your typical audience

_____You can bring diverse expectations together

## Produce your Message

____You know precisely the outcome of each presentation

____You can summarize your message in 25 words

____You know how to tell a business story

____All your key messages are tagged

## Make your Connection

____You know how to instantly build rapport

____You have methods to hold your audience's attention

____Your presentations are highly interactive

____You are regarded as an engaging presenter

## Deliver with Style

____You are happy with your current vocal variety

____You know how to use eye contact to engage an audience

____Your body language is totally in tune with your delivery

____You are content with your slide presentations

## Manage all Interruptions

____You handle all interruptions with ease

____You can operate confidently in a room of any size

____You know how to limit disruptions to your presentation

## Master the Q&A

____The question and answer session is your favorite part

____You are confident running a Q&A session

____You handle every question with ease, even difficult ones

## Finish on Time

____You know how to rehearse effectively

____You remain confident when your presenting time gets cut in half

Take a look at the statements you answered with N or NS, and for those sections that you have answered with three or more, go to those chapters first. Pick up tips you can use immediately for your next presentation. Many of the tips take one minute to read and apply.

Some areas may take longer to improve. Make a weekly plan to try out new tips and techniques as you present and communicate with people around you.

# B. Be Yourself

Being authentic is an essential part of becoming a *One Minute Presenter*. It's about finding your own speaking voice and being able to naturally and comfortably communicate back and forward with an audience.

To be yourself as a presenter you need to:

- Talk about your family roots and background
- Share your beliefs and values
- Share your passion for your subject
- Talk about real challenges and lessons you have learned
- Be honest and straightforward
- Be consistent
- Have fun appropriately
- Have confidence

As you work your way through this book, and while you're preparing for your next presentation, think about ways you can add more of yourself into the speech.

First, learn the skills of a *One Minute Presenter* from the 8 stations. Second, start to add more of "yourself" into your presentations as you increase your competency. Enjoy the journey!

# C. Become Fearless

## Survival fear

Survival fear is the classic "flight or fight" response all animals (yes, you're an animal!) have when faced with perceived danger. Adrenaline is released, eyes widen, muscles tightened, sweating results, and heart rate increases. This was first described by Walter Cannon in 1915 and he found all animals react to threats in similar ways. The adrenaline helps get the body ready for physical exertion either to run away from the danger or to stand and fight back. You may have felt this if you have been in a dangerous situation. I went to a circus when I was 7 years old and one of the elephants escaped during the show. As the big elephant ran through the audience (past the Royal box where Princess Anne was sitting), you could see survival fear spread around the tent. Most chose flight. Luckily, so did the elephant and apart from knocking over a few chairs there was no damage. Some presenters do get a very strong physical reaction before presenting and we'll look at techniques to work through this later in this chapter.

## Conditioned fear

Conditioned fear has two main types: learned fear and traumatic fear. With learned fear, a person can be conditioned to fear an object that is not necessarily dangerous. In psychology, fear conditioning was first tested in 1920 by an experiment

## WHAT CAUSES FEAR?

Fear is an emotional response to threats and danger. There are two types of fear. One type is natural: *survival fear*.

The second is learned: *conditioned fear*. This occurs when we have bad experiences and wish not to repeat them. Most presenters need help with the second type.

## IS FEAR GOOD OR BAD?

Fear is an emotional response that triggers different types of emotional reaction depending on the perceived threat. The amygdala is the key brain structure involved in the processing of negative emotions such as fear and anger. The amygdala is an ancient part of the brain and can be traced back to our reptilian ancestry. This automatic response blocks conscious thought. While in life or death situations this is extremely useful, in our day to day tasks it reduces our ability to work effectively. Unless we can consciously be aware of what is causing us to feel fear, we'll be ruled by our fear.

called the Little Albert experiment. By today's standards this experiment is unethical. In summary, an 11-month-old boy was conditioned to fear a white rat in the laboratory although the boy had not previously feared the rat and was comfortable in handling and playing with the rat.

## Overcoming traumatic experiences

The second type of conditioned fear is caused by traumatic accidents. For example, if a child swallowed water while learning to swim, it's possible they will learn to fear water or swimming or even taking a boat. The reason many people "fear" presenting is due to a traumatic past experience. When I was 11 years old, I had to act out a role on stage for a drama class that resulted in me crying in front of the whole class (ouch!). This conditioned me to associate speaking out in public with great pain, and I went to any length to avoid it for 18 years. Whenever I had to give a presentation, it would be with a pounding heart, dry mouth and sweaty hands. Eventually I got over this fear and discovered my passion for public speaking. One of my motivations for writing this book is to help you shortcut your learning curve and not wait (18 years) to become the great presenter that you can become.

Think back. Have you had a negative past experience while speaking (or singing) in public that may be causing your fear today?

# Nerves don't go away, fear does

Once we have our fear under control, we may think that the nerves will disappear too. That's not always the case and many presenters still get pre-presentation jitters. Even seasoned presenters still feel the butterflies in their stomach after many years of presenting. Famous performers such as Clint Eastwood, Sir Laurence Olivier and Forest Whitaker all suffered from stage fright. If you do still feel the nerves, use this energy and channel it into your presentation.

This table shows common symptoms you may feel before a presentation:

| Signs you may fear presenting in public |
| --- |
| **Signs only visible to you** |
| • Hands sweating, heart beating, body shaking, numb legs, dry mouth, blank mind |
| • Embarrassed just at the thought of speaking in public |
| • Zero confidence |
| • Fear from past bad experiences come to mind |
| • Panic when asked to deliver a presentation at work |
| **Signs visible to others** |
| • Difficult to look audience in the eye |
| • Make apologies before/during/after presentation |
| • Look down at feet or up at the ceiling during presentation |
| • Rush through presentation without pausing, or asking questions to the audience |
| • Talk down your credentials while presenting |
| • Tell audience you are not prepared |
| • Speak faster than you normally would |
| • Face or ears turn red |

Now we understand what fear is, we need some tools to help us overcome its negative affects. Here are six fearbusters to help you overcome and fight the fear. They don't involve food, alcohol or drugs which evade the source of the fear and are short term unhealthy fixes.

## Fearbuster#1: Work your body

The first step in beating nerves, stress or a bad mood is a good physical condition. Water and oxygen are a great way to keep a healthy body. Imagine yourself standing on top of a mountain looking around breathing in fresh clean mountain air and sipping a bottle of cool clean spring water. You get the picture. It's making me feel more relaxed already. Now you may not have the benefit of a mountain nearby, so what else can you do? Exercise. My business coach picked this out during one of our sessions. He noticed that whenever I was down on life in general, it was usually at the same time as a drop in my exercising. His solution was to swim, run and cycle more. It worked for me as I love triathlon racing. Here's how it can work for you too:

1. Have a workout during the week of your presentation. Block out the time and spend two hours doing whatever exercise you enjoy most. Go for a swim, take a run or visit a gym. Finish off with a spa or massage if you have time.

2. On the day of your presentation, take a walk to get some air in your lungs, which improves your blood circulation and controls your nerves. See Fearbuster#4 for more on breathing.

3. A few hours before your presentation avoid drinking tea, coffee or caffeine based soft drinks (including colas). These are diuretics which remove water from your body. You should drink plenty of water as this has a calming effect by making your body aerobic.

4. Just before you come on stage, walk out your nerves. Don't sit down just before coming on stage. Get the blood moving so you're coming in at a higher energy level. You can also stretch your neck, shoulders, arms and fingers to relax any tense muscles. Meeting and greeting your audience can help you transform nervous energy and start to create a connection.

## Fearbuster#2: Help a friend

This may seem a paradox as before a presentation, you're very focused on yourself, your performance and what could go wrong. Snap yourself out of this self focus by looking around and seeing how you can help someone. You may help with the meeting room set-up, give out agendas or flyers. Talk with the meeting facilitator or host and ask them if they are ready. By switching attention to help someone else, you're doing two very important things. Firstly, you're shifting your attention away from being too self centered. Secondly, you're shifting your energy towards helping. Let's face it: we all like that feeling when we help someone. If you want to imagine the difference in energy, think of Donald Trump and Mother Teresa. The "Donald" brand personifies competition, while the Mother Teresa brand embodies helping others. You no doubt feel differently when you think of these two (incredible) people. While you're building up your confidence, start with the intention of helping others. This will help you become more sincere and lower your nerves in your presentation. You don't need to be Mother Teresa to give a good presentation. Just remember that you're helping others deepen their understanding on your topic. You are doing a service. You are helping.

## Fearbuster#3: Visualising for success: get mentally prepared

Ancient wisdom tells us we tend to get the things we think about most and give the most energy to. So when you're very nervous and thinking about all the things which could go wrong in your presentations, you're setting yourself up for failure. At the very least you will not enjoy the experience. Like professional sports stars, we need to visualize success before we get out in front of an audience. It works for Tiger Woods. After Tiger shot a 28 on nine holes (to non golfers, that's an amazing score!) during the second round of the Tour Championship in Florida, his caddie reported that Tiger was using visualization in the run up to the tournament to improve his swing. It can work for you. This four-step process can help you get mentally prepared:

## a. Remember your past successes

You don't need to think about a presentation. Imagine serving aces if you like tennis, or scoring a goal if football is your sport. Hear the audience roar with appreciation and applaud loudly at your success. The more dramatic and emotional you can make your success picture, the more effective it will be. If you don't like sports, just choose another time when you were successful, like passing an important examination or driving test. Recall the feeling of pleasure and satisfaction. Bring this feeling into your presentation. We all have success stories. Put these images in your mind and remind yourself how it felt to be a success. See the successful outcome. Hear the congratulations you received. Feel the joy of being a success. Think about any time you have been successful. Here are some examples:

| | |
|---|---|
| Getting a job you wanted | Passing an exam |
| Getting a boyfriend or girlfriend | Getting into a good school |
| Being made a leader at school or work | Passing your high school exam |
| Graduating from university | Reaching a stretch target |
| Meeting your dream man or woman | Having your first child |
| Feeling after working out or swimming | Feeling after a good meal you have cooked for your family |
| Feeling of climbing to the top of a mountain | Signing a big contract |

## b. Build up the feeling

Remember how it felt at that time. Remember the excitement, the feeling of achievement and success. As you think about this moment, you should notice that your heart is beating a little faster. You should be able to feel the energy in your body as you remember this high point of your life. This is the type of image you should have in your mind before presenting. Visualize the appreciation of a happy audience. See the audience being receptive to your presentation. Perhaps some are nodding their heads, others are smiling and taking notes. Feel the respect and satisfaction you get from giving the audience exactly what they want to hear. Think back to previous successful presentations you have given and recall the feeling you got then.

## c. Bring to present moment

Now, with these successful images and sounds in your mind, take a couple of breaths and imagine the audience you're about to face. They are smiling. They are welcoming you. They applaud. They accept your message. They love you. You are a great person. You are successful.

## d. Confirm your success

The final step is to reinforce your success with a short slogan. To end your visualization you can repeat a short slogan with energy so you're now ready to present with enthusiasm.

## SHOULD I IMAGINE MY AUDIENCE NAKED?

One myth to bust. Over the years I have heard people recommend you imagine your audience sitting undressed or partially dressed. Perhaps this is due to Winston Churchill's quote that he imagined his audience sitting naked in order to reduce his nerves. But personally I wouldn't recommend this as it can start to distract you! Focus on the outcome of your presentation, which is to deliver your message with style to an engaged audience. Not, I hope, to have an undressed audience. It may work if you're a rap singer, like Jay-Z, but for most business presentations this could just be a distraction.

**Some examples:**

*"I'm going to deliver a great presentation."*

*"I'm delivering a totally successful presentation."*

*"I'm the best presenter in the world."*

*"This presentation is going to be a total success."*

Have fun with it. Exaggerate a little bit if it helps you build up your energy!

# Fearbuster#4: Deep rhythmical breathing

Getting a steady supply of oxygen can help calm those nerves. Deep breathing is the most convenient way to get this (unless you have an oxygen tank!). You don't need a quiet room, a yoga mat or new age music. The best breathing exercises can be done anywhere and anytime you need to calm down. I use them when I'm stuck in traffic. Try them before an important phone call or meeting, or anytime you're waiting around with nothing to do: in the elevator, on the train platform, in the car. Here is a basic effective breathing exercise:

1. Breathe in deeply through your nose. Your stomach should fill with air and push out slightly. Count to three.

2. Breathe out through your mouth while your stomach pulls in. Count to three.

3. Repeat this five times. Then as you get used to it, try ten times.

The more you use it, the more effective it becomes. It's so simple that you can use it anytime you need to relax. You can also add positive words to the breathing if that works for you. Try this one from Vietnamese Zen master, Thich Nhat Hanh: *"Breathing in, I calm my body. Breathing out, I smile."*

# Fearbuster#5: Find a support group

Have you ever asked the wrong people for advice? I have. When I was thinking about setting up as a professional presentation skills trainer, I asked my friends and family if they thought it was a good idea for me to leave my corporate training position in a Big 4 accounting firm. I had some encouraging words from mum (naturally!) and some mixed advice from friends. My graphic designer (at the time) told me that she couldn't imagine there was any need for this service! Luckily, I also found a group of entrepreneurs. They were more encouraging and could actually relate to the decision I was going through as many of them had taken similar choices before setting up their own companies. You need to find a support group. Have a supportive network of people who don't share the same fear as you. If you have a fear of public speaking, it's better to go and find people that have already conquered that fear. If you had a fear of flying, you wouldn't want to be around a bunch of similar people every time you had to board a plane.

Fear generates fear. So make sure the people around you are not contributing to your fear of public speaking. An organization I heartily recommend is Toastmasters International. In my opinion, there is no better place to go to get over the fear of public speaking. With 235,000 members in 11,700 clubs in 92 countries, this 84-year-old non-profit organization has helped many people (myself included) turn nerves into applause with their step by step approach and supportive environment. See **www.toastmasters.org** for a club near you.

**BE PREPARED**

Robert Baden-Powell is famous for his "be prepared" advice to scouts. Knowing your content inside out and rehearsing it before you deliver will increase your confidence and lower anxiety.

# Fearbuster#6: Hire a learning coach

If you're looking to improve in big jumps (rather than little steps), find yourself a coach. In my life, I have had a maths coach, music coach, tennis coach, swimming coach, language coach, life coach, business coach and many more. Having a guide, mentor or teacher is essential to fast tracking your learning in any field. There are no original mistakes to make because someone has already made the mistakes you're making today. If you can learn how to jump over these potential pitfalls before they happen, you're accelerating your learning. Learn by doing is an effective way to learn (and this is how Toastmasters learn), but you can't beat learning from a master. Every major sports star in the Olympics has a coach. Look into finding a coach near you. The professional speakers associations can be a great place to find a speaking mentor. See the Resources section at the back of this book.

## Next chapter

The next stop in *The One Minute Presenter's* journey is "Treasure your Audience", where you learn how to paint a portrait of your ideal audience and manage diverse expectations.

# − 5 −

# Treasure your Audience

"Three quarters of the miseries and misunderstandings in the world would finish if people were to put on the shoes of their adversaries and understood their points of view."

*Mahatma Gandhi, Indian philosopher, esteemed for his doctrine of nonviolent protest, 1869-1948.*

## This chapter's content:

▶ A. Portrait your audience.
*Page 44*

▶ B. Create a golden avatar.
*Page 47*

▶ C. Value diverse expectations.
*Page 52*

## One Minute Learning:

● How to paint a portrait of your audience
*Page 44*

● Understand the difference between demographics and psychographics
*Page 44*

● Techniques to gather information about your audience
*Page 45*

● How to create an avatar of your ideal audience
*Page 47*

● Essential questions to build up a golden avatar profile
*Page 48*

● Why today's audience expectations are so diverse
*Page 52*

● Four reasons an audience wants to listen to you
*Page 53*

● How to create a perspective that starts from the audience's interests
*Page 54*

## Process:

☞ First, make a portrait of your audience so you understand who your audience is and what their motivations are.

☞ Second, create a golden avatar of your ideal audience so you personalize your audience and give them a name and personality.

☞ Third, ready yourself to face an audience of diverse expectations.

# Case study#2:
## *Mike, marketing manager, consumer goods.*

Mike was identified as a high performing talent in a large multinational and was recently promoted to brand development manager requiring a shift in portfolio and reporting lines. He now needed to give about twice as many presentations as before to both his business unit and regionally to colleagues and senior management. As Mike stepped into another presentation he often asked himself the question *"Who is in my audience today?"*

It was hard to keep track, as he seldom got sufficient information on the audience's background. Mike often faced situations where he had to present to senior management from different disciplines, who had differing levels of interest in the details of his presentation. It was a struggle sometimes to find the right level of detail to present. *"How can I deal with these diverse expectations? How can I understand my audience?"*

Mike felt he was not quite able to connect and understand his audience's needs and issues at this level. It was certainly harder than his previous role as product manager. He noticed in these presentations, he was unable to hold the attention of his audience for very long and key decision makers were distracted by outside messages and often stepped out of the room never to return. He was starting to become frustrated with his role and was starting to think more seriously about the offers he frequently received from headhunters.

This chapter helps you understand your audience more deeply and prepares you to face an audience with mixed expectations.

# A. Portrait your Audience

### How can I understand my audience?

In art, a portrait is a likeness of a person's face and the purpose is usually to express their personality and mood. The world's oldest known portrait is 27,000 years old in a cave in France. Since then portraits have played an important part of human expression from Roman sculptures to the Mona Lisa. This technique can be very useful when preparing for an audience. Building a portrait of your audience gives your audience a "face". Software developers use portraits when designing user interfaces as this helps them understand the expectations a typical "experienced" user or "newbie" user would have on a software interface. It's also a popular technique for marketers who want to build a profile for their customers.

A portrait will start with looking at your audience's demographics and psychographics.

Example of a basic audience portrait:

| Demographics | Psychographics |
|---|---|
| What you can see & easily measure | What you can't see & can't easily measure |
| Location | How they spend their workdays. |
| Age | What they care about. |
| Nationality | Lifestyle values. |
| Occupation | Attitudes to important issues (environment). |
| Level in the organization | Member of sub-cultures. |

As part of your research, you should begin with demographics to narrow the field. Then you need to spend more time to learn about the psychographics, which ultimately, will make your talk more personable. In the case study, when Mike started addressing the psychographic needs of his audience, he became a more engageing presenter.

Think of it like online dating. While you can punch in all your physical information about age, height, weight and physical appearance and so on, this is not going to result in a good match (well unlikely). It's only when you add in the interests, lifestyles, attitudes and values that you can start to make a connection with someone. The reason online dating is so popular is because it helps narrow the field in an efficient way, so people can spend more time working out the tricky part - the psychographics!

Investing time to deepen your understanding of your audience's psychographic portrait will reap high dividends. Here are some techniques to get this information:

- Visit web sites and intranets to learn more about your audience (and also about their customers)

- Talk to a colleague who has already presented to this audience and ask them VAL questions

- Call a sample of participants before the presentation to get a feeling for what they're interested in learning from your presentation

- Understand the business pains your audience is currently suffering

- Learn about the business objectives and expectations they have for this year

- Walk to their department (if practical) and see how they work

- Take an opinion leader to lunch to deepen your understanding of their motivations

## Here are some questions to guide you:

- How much do they know about your subject?

- How much detail will they expect (technical or business focused)?

- What's their attitude to you, your department and your objectives?

- What "hot topic" will get their attention?

- What five "burning questions" would your audience like to ask you?

By collecting these valuable insights your audience becomes like an old friend, willing and ready to greet your presentation. Once you have a portrait of your audience, you can refine it and deepen your understanding for the audience's motivations. The next important step is to create a golden avatar.

# B. Create a Golden Avatar

*How well do you know your audience?*

It's no surprise the audience is the most important part of your presentation because nothing happens without audience approval and acceptance. But how well do you know your audience? Can you "see" them? Do you know what's on their mind?

This section will look at ways to create a personality for your audience. We call it the Golden Avatar to remind you how important understanding your audience is for your business presenting success.

One technique you can use is to create an avatar of your core or typical audience.

## Why should I create an avatar for my audience?

Whether your audience is a client, an employee or a stakeholder, you need to know more about them. By creating an avatar or character, you're making them real, giving them a personality. You can start to imagine sitting having a coffee with them in Starbucks or grabbing lunch. This is important because a bunch of demographic data, while nice to have, doesn't help you connect with your audience. Your client avatar means you can imagine them as a real person (which they are) and get comfortable with their needs, desires and attitudes before you get into the presentation. Here's how you can create an avatar:

## WHAT'S AN AVATAR?

An avatar (orginally a Sanskrit word, Avatara, meaning "incarnation") has been used in the computing world since the 1980s and is a **character** a person takes on while playing a computer game, instant messaging or in virtual worlds such as Second Life.

## Exercise:

1. Take a typical audience you present to.

2. Answer the avatar creation questions below.

3. Build a profile for your avatar.

4. Name your avatar (eg "Bob" or "Mary").

5. Imagine giving your presentation to Bob or Mary and see how this helps you connect with them.

## Avatar creation questions:

- What are they called?

- Who do they think they are?

- Who are they really?

- Who do they want to be?

- Who do they like?

- Who don't they like?

- Who is their peer group?

- Who do they not identify with?

- What are their beliefs?

- Where do they live?

- Where do they work?

- Where do they learn?

- Where do they want to be?

- What are their needs?

- How old are they?

- How youthful do they act?

- How conservative are they?

- What are their driving ambitions?

- What are their wants and needs?

- What are their pleasures?

- What are their pains?

- What do they love?

- What do they hate?

*Avatar questions courtesy of Chris Garrett, who is a professional blogger, internet marketing consultant, new media industry commentator, writer, coach, speaker, trainer and web geek. He was also a founding member of Performancing. See more about Chris at www.chrisg.com.*

# Create a character

Build on your avatar by using character creating techniques used by authors and screenplay writers. These are not all the questions you can ask and answer about your characters but this will definitely provide you with a solid foundation to develop and create them. Pick and choose questions which help you build up a more detailed picture of your audience.

## Their background

- What year were they born and where?
- What's the most exciting thing that ever happened to them?

## Their interests

- What sport(s) do they love to play? Watch?
- What's their favorite movie? TV show? Music?
- What's their favorite color?
- What's their favorite food? Beverage?
- Do they gamble?
- What are their hobbies? Interests?
- What makes them laugh? Cry? What makes them sad? Angry?

## Their career

- How do they make a living?

## Their family

- Are they married? Have they ever been? Do they believe in marriage?
- Do they have children? Do they like children?
- Do they have a brother and / or sister?
- Was their childhood strict? Lenient?
- What was their families economic status?

## Their personality

- What are three character flaws?
- Are they aggressive? Passive?

- How do they show or protect their feelings?
- How do they get along with other people?

## Their appearance

- What's their strongest physical attribute?
- How do they dress?

## Their role model

- Who in the world would they change places with if they could?
- Who is their favorite actor and or actress?

## Their lifestyle

- What's their health like?
- What type of house or apartment do they live in? How is it furnished?
- Do they smoke or drink alcohol?
- Do they read the newspaper? Books? Magazines?
- Do they work out? Are they energetic? Sluggish?

## Their aspirations

- If they could change one thing about the world what would it be?
- What's their goal in life?

## Their attitudes

- How do they feel about the opposite sex? The same sex?
- What's their outlook on life? Positive? Negative?
- What's their self image? How do they feel about their own size? Looks? Weight? Height?
- How do they deal with hostility? Negativity? Ridicule?

This greater knowledge about your audience will give you more confidence while you present. Over time you will become an expert on presenting to your target audience. You will still need to keep flexible because today's audiences are diverse.

# C. Value Diverse Expectations

**How can I deal with diverse expectations?**

Today your audience is different from what it was five years ago. Due to a number of macro or global changes, you're facing a much more diverse audience. Here are some of those big picture trends:

| From | To |
| --- | --- |
| Mass market | Niche market |
| Homogenous (same) needs | Hetergenous (diverse) needs |
| Same attitudes | Diverse attitudes |
| Local | Global |
| Few segments | Many segments |
| Offline | Online |
| Fixed | Mobile |
| Inhuman | Human |

What this means is it's harder for you to relate to the audience. They're more diverse and not even age, sex and nationality are accurate predictors of attitudes, needs and desires anymore. You face a mixed room. Let's see how expectations can diverge in a presentation for a new product launch.

Your presentation may need to include information on a new programming code you are using. If your audience is fellow software programmers, you will need a lot of technical details because your audience are closer to the subject. However, in the same room, a finance manager may be sitting there waiting for the financial projections. A senior manager joins to learn about the business case. The marketing team want to know about how this product fits into the current portfolio. You must balance the technical details (which you may enjoy) and consider how other important stakeholders would like to digest the information they need to hear. You will need to cut out the tech stuff and focus on end uses, business benefits and you will need to do so in a non-technical and jargon-free way. Doing your homework before the meeting and painting a portrait of the complete audience will put you in a very strong position.

## Skeptical audiences

Living in an information rich world, we have access to knowledge from the best experts in the world. In fact, unlike the "dark ages" before the internet, we have freer and easier access to the world's best knowledge than any other generation. So we have heard a lot of good advice. We have heard the tips, insights, secrets and sharings of the best gurus, rainmakers and marketers. Here lies the paradox. There is a big gap between knowing and doing. Between saying and doing. So we tend to say, "*Yes, I know.*" When really what we mean is, "*Yes. I have heard about it, but I haven't actually done it.*"

In an age of fast food, fast technology and fast education, we have really forgotten what lies beneath the success of today's billionaires. Get beneath the massive brand name of Donald Trump and you find a man with a massive work ethic, and a deep understanding of his industry.

## Make your diverse audience whole again

One of the purposes of presenting to an audience is to help them solve this "hard work." Every presentation you give should help the audience:

1. Solve a problem

2. Meet a need

3. Reach a goal

4. Answer a question

You need to see this from the audience's perspective by saying "SWIIFY" – "*So What's In It For You?*"

This is where most presenters lose the audience. They focus on the wrong "you". The "you" is your audience (not the presenter) and what they want to experience, learn and discover.

## YOU NEED TO LOVE, HONOUR AND RESPECT YOUR AUDIENCE

Do you have unconditional love for your audience? Do you know what they care about? Being audience focused means you don't have any assumptions about your audience. You need to identify who your audience is, discover what's important to them and what they care about, what makes them unique. Lovemarks, invented by Kevin Roberts CEO of global advertising agency Saatchi & Saatchi, capture the essence of attracting today's audiences. Lovemarks transcend brands, fads and products by commanding both love and respect.

*Learn more at www.lovemarks.com.*

| From | To |
|------|-----|
| Me | You |
| I want... | What you want is ... |
| Features (that I think are great) | Benefits (that you would like to enjoy) |
| The whole story | The highlights (what matters most to you) |
| Official, formal and important | Personal, relaxed and friendly |
| It's not about you | It's about them |

Once you have your SWIIFYs, you can link them to the audience during your presentation:

- *So, this is important to you because...*
- *What this means for you is..*
- *Why is this important? Here's why...*

The more you focus on the audience's needs (SWIIFYs), the more they will listen to and stay focused on your message.

### Next chapter

Now you have a deep understanding of your target audience. So what do you want to say to them? We're going to go to Bollywood and Hollywood and look at happy endings, making a movie message and sound biting your key phrases. Let's look at how you can "Produce your Message".

# – 6 –

## THE THIRD STATION:

# Produce your Message

"Wise men speak because they have something to say; fools because they have to say something."

*Plato, Ancient Greek philosopher.*

## This chapter's content:

▶ A. Happy endings.
*Page 58*

▶ B. Make a movie message.
*Page 62*

▶ C. Tell a business story.
*Page 65*

▶ D. Tag your message.
*Page 68*

## One Minute Learning:

● Define a clear end-point for your presentation
*Page 58*

● Write your high concept (your message in a nutshell)
*Page 62*

● Personalize your content using storytelling
*Page 65*

● Make taglines with slogans and soundbites
*Page 68*

## Process:

☞ First, write a 25-word happy ending that summarizes what you want your audience to think, feel and do at the end of your presentation.

☞ Second, think like a movie producer to turn your presentation into a concept that can be used in a variety of different presentations.

☞ Third, use characters to make your content come alive by using a 5-step business storytelling process.

☞ Fourth, pick out key parts of your speech and like a good TV reporter turn them into soundbites and slogans, which become the taglines of your message.

# Case study#3:
## *Dave, sales engineer, software industry.*

Dave has been a sales person and sales engineer for a long time. Over the years, he has learned to be flexible. He has had many experiences where presentation topics get changed on the day. As a result, Dave has learned to be ready for a broad range of subjects. Sometimes the customer is the one making the change and sometimes it's the sales team failing to keep him informed.

Recently, as part of his personal development plan, Dave decided to get some feedback on his presentation skills from a group of his colleagues. The feedback was written and people were asked to express exactly what they thought. Dave scored pretty well on overall delivery and very high on technical ability. He was able to be credible as an expert due to his experience. Some interesting comments were made in his "areas to improve" feedback cards:

*I'm not really sure where the presentation is going.*

*What are you trying to say? Get to the point.*

*I can't see the benefits here. So dry and boring.*

*The long list of points was really weak. I wasn't sure what the key point was.*

Dave took this feedback and realized his past experiences meant he tended to be too general in his approach to topics. When he became aware of the negative impact it had, he decided to produce a more focused message.

This chapter looks at the steps you can take to make an audience-focused message.

# A. Happy Endings

Let's learn the importance of having a super clear picture of where you want to take your audience during your presentation. As author of *The 7 Habits of Highly Effective People*, Dr. Stephen Covey said, *"Begin with the end in mind."* Let's see how this relates to presentations.

## What's my destination?

A creative media friend used to enjoy her afternoons by going to a bus stop, jumping on the first bus, and riding it around until she came to a place where it seemed like a nice place to get off. She often ended up in completely strange and unusual places miles from anywhere she knew. Have you ever done that? I bet you haven't. The idea of getting on a bus without knowing where you're going seems crazy to most people. And perhaps it is. It's like trying to buy a train ticket without knowing where you want to go.

Do your presentations have a clear destination, or are you driving your audience around from stop to stop, not really knowing where you're going?

Every good presentation, like a relaxing bus journey, has a clear outcome or destination. No surprises. You know where you're going from the moment you get on. No unexpected detours. No random turns down side streets. And hopefully no breakdowns. If you have ever left a presentation asking yourself, *"What was that all about?"*, you have experienced a presentation without a happy ending.

## Your happy ending is your destination

Your happy ending is the destination you would like to take your audience to at the end of the presentation. If your presentation was a bus, your happy ending would be the place where the audience gets off at the end of the journey.

You need to have a clear happy ending in mind as you prepare your content. Everything will hook onto your happy ending. All content will support you in reaching this objective or goal. Take a minute and think about a recent presentation you have given. Write down your happy ending.

An effective happy ending is written down. It should be about 20-25 words and cover 3 main areas. The "3H's": head, heart and hands. In other words, what do you want your audience to think, feel and do by the time your presentation finishes? If you're not sure how to write your happy ending, you can write down the "3Hs" separately. Then re-write them into a single happy ending. Let's show how this works with an example.

## Create a happy ending

This process works for any audience. Let's take a sales situation. You are presenting to a client. Your "happy ending" is to gain agreement for your proposal.

### "Think with your head"

What do you want your client to think during and at the end of your presentation?

### "Feel with your heart"

What do you want your client to feel during and at the end of your presentation?

### "Do with your hands"

What do you want your client to do during and at the end of your presentation?

**At the end of my presenta-
tion, my client will...**

...think we are competent,
capable and ideally suited to
help them. Feel comfortable
in our communication styles,
and select a project start date
(24 words).

## Some possibilities include:

### "Think with your head"

*I want my client to think we are competent, capable
and ideally suited to help them.*

*I want my client to think we understand their business
situation and we are committed to help them improve
it.*

*I want my client to think we are easy to work with and
have the resources to provide excellent service.*

### "Feel with your heart"

*I want my client to feel confident in our capabilities.*

*I want my client to feel confident that the outcomes of
the proposal will be delivered.*

*I want my client to feel comfortable in our communi-
cation styles.*

*I want my client to feel we are the best choice.*

### "Do with your hands"

*I want my client to express confirmation that the pro-
ject objectives are in line with their expectations.*

*I want my client to understand the proposal options
and indicate a preference.*

*I want my client to select a start date for the project.*

*I want my client to map out the next steps we take
following the meeting.*

# Clearer outcomes are effective

Delivering an effective presentation requires a clear idea of the destination. The clearer you are about where you want to take the audience, the better your chance of taking them there. Write down your happy ending before each presentation, and after each presentation ask yourself how well you did in reaching the planned destination.

Once you have a clear outcome to take your audience, you need to decide how you will get there. This vehicle is your message. We'll now examine the three essential components of every robust message and how to integrate your message throughout your presentation. We'll look at three levels to design your message:

- Make a movie message
  (high level message)

- Tell a business story
  (ground level message)

- Tagline your message
  (mid level message)

A great resource for excellent business communication is *"Your Attention, please"*.

Authors Davis and Brown explain why today's audiences are more distracted than ever before and provide a rich variety of ways to appeal to them.

*See more at www. yourattentionpleasebook.com.*

# B. Make a Movie Message

The high level message is your message in a nutshell. It's the shortest possible way to express your message so that your audience understands where you will be taking them.

## Follow Spielberg's advice

In movie making, the high level message is also known as the "high concept". The 1979 science fiction movie Aliens had a very concise high concept: "Jaws on a spaceship"- especially relevant following the 1975 runaway success of the first Jaws movie. That movie's director Steven Spielberg once said, *"If a person can tell me the idea in 25 words or less, it's going to make a pretty good movie."*

## Use a high concept

This technique is used by those heavyweights of persuasive communications in Hollywood (movies), Madison Avenue (advertising), and Washington (politics). And you can use it too.

The high concept for *The One Minute Presenter* is:

*Busy business executives become masters of engaging presentations through a systematic process of connecting carefully crafted and produced messages with today's most distracted, inattentive audiences. (25 words)*

## Your flexible friend

It may not win any Oscars but it gets the happy ending across in 25 words. Why would you want to concisely say your message in 25 words or less? Here comes the great part. If you understand why this part is so essential, so vital to presenting today, then you're well on the way to becoming a *One Minute Presenter*. If you can define your message in 25 words or less, your message can be used to fit any given situation. If you express your message in such a concise manner, you can be confident in expressing yourself in every possible communication situation. For example:

- A chat with your boss in an elevator

- Over coffee with a colleague

- In an interview with a potential hire

- In a networking event with a prospect

- During a five-minute keynote to regional management

- In full, during a 30 minute presentation

*The One Minute Presenter* is always ready. Your high concept is the key to always being ready.

## How to make a high concept

You will need to go through several rounds of edits before you can create a short meaningful concept. Here is an example of how we did this with *"The One Minute Presenter."*

| 34 words | You, the presenter must treasure your audience to produce your message. Once you create your connection, you can deliver with style {with technology}, manage all interruptions, master the Q&A to finish on time. |
| --- | --- |
| 25 words | Busy business executives become masters of engaging presentations through a systematic process of connecting carefully crafted and produced messages with today's most distracted, inattentive audiences. |
| 10 words | Executives master how to engage even the most inattentive audiences. |

## Concise is memorable

Your message can now be recycled to fit any given situation. This clarity of conciseness is what today's busy audiences crave. The more comprehensive you are, the less effective you become. The more data you pile on and the more slides you flip through, the more likely your audience is to be completely overwhelmed and ultimately forget whatever message you have delivered.

### A quick checklist for making your movie message:

1. Is it clear and simple?

2. Is it to the point?

3. Do you know where the "journey" is heading?

4. Is it 25 words or less?

# C. Tell a Business Story

It's a human need to listen to and share stories. From children's bedtime tales, to the billion dollar Hollywood movies and now with blogs, internet chats and Twitters, it's all about sharing stories. We love to be entertained and enjoy the emotions a good story can arouse from excitement, love, and laughter. A good story touches the heart.

When Google launched their open source browser Chrome, they used an online comic book story to explain the benefits of the new browser through a cast of characters. This approach took a complex subject and made it more accessible and easier to understand. See the story online by googling "Google Chrome comic book".

## Remember the story...

At the same time, a good story will communicate important knowledge to the audience. Think of Aesop's fables – children's short stories about animals. *The hare and tortoise* and *The wolf in sheep's clothing* are entertaining while educating important life lessons. The Chinese have used fables for thousands of years to educate children on doing the right thing.

## ...and you remember the message

A good story communicates the moral indirectly – rather than hitting the audience over the head with the message. Unfortunately, hitting people over the head with a message can also be effective – think political messages and advertisements for dubious medical products. Unfortunately repetition does work in the short run – even for tacky advertising.

But let's assume your audience is a little more sophisticated. In business, the Harvard Business Review is famous for its case study, which highlights a business through the use of a story and feedback from experts. And if it works for them, it can work for you too. Every good story has a number of fixed elements.

# Elements of a business story

1. Is audience focused.

2. Has a single message.

3. Follows the rule of three – an opening, a body and a close:
   - Opening introduces the characters and the obstacles
   - Body deals with the problems
   - Close brings together a resolution

4. Has believable characters.

5. Uses facts (who, what, where, when, why, how).

6. Creates tension.

# Story check list

1) Do you have a movie message?

2) What is your happy ending?

3) Where does your story begin?

4) Why is this topic important now?

5) What's the tipping point?

6) What likable hero will the audience relate with?

7) What "villain" can represent your challenge?

8) What is your hero's motivation?

# Make it more specific

Big words may make you feel important, but they also tend to be vague and abstract. Specific is good. Abstract not so much. Think of presenting like flying at 10,000 meters. When you look out of a the window at 10,000 meters everything on the ground is out of focus. You can't make out any detail – you can just see a blur: some green over there, seems like a freeway over there. Are those houses or a shopping mall?

Using big, important words can be like presenting at 10,000 meters. Even if your audience can follow you, the message seems blurry and vague. They leave the presentation saying, *"Great presentation, but what was the message?"* or *"I got the general idea, but not sure what that means for me."*

Every time you present, you need to make sure you present from the ground level. Give the details and paint a complete picture so there is no doubt about the picture - your message.

You need to use word-pictures which include the five senses. You need to lead your audience through the presentation like a demonstration or journey, step by step. Think of those TV infomercials demonstrating how to use an exercise bike step by step, leaving no one in any doubt about what the benefits could be. They use male and female perspectives, they show how professionals could use and even the absolute beginners. They show people of all ages using it. Even if you had never thought about using an exercise bike, after a few minutes you're thinking, *"You know, I could really use one of them."* That is a successful presentation. So how can *your* communication become more specific?

## Your message should be short and simple

**Short.** Look around you and things are getting shorter. Books are getting shorter. TV sound bites are getting shorter (8 seconds or less). Movie cuts are getting more frequent. A newspaper article is now around 300 words in USA Today. And new media like Twitter and Facebook encourage very short communication styles. Cut out unnecessary points, slides and words. Use short words over long.

**Simple.** Today's attention deficit audiences need simplicity if you expect them to pay attention. Choose easy to understand words. Cut out the jargon. Explain people, places and things. Don't assume the audience has the same knowledge and perspective as you. Think of your role as someone who is helping the audience cut through the hardshell of information surrounding them, and showing them the sweet, concise and relevant parts to them.

# D. Tag your Message

The above three tips will help you produce a compelling message. To take this to a higher level, you need to tag your message. Creating taglines for your overall presentation and key sub-sections will help you (and the audience) memorize your important messages and allow you flexibility in your delivery. This advanced skill is similar to the branding approach used in advertising and marketing today.

In Chapter 1 we learned about the massive information overload swamping us daily. This has turned words into a cheap commodity. There is a surplus of words in the world. A complete glut. If words had a stock, they would be a penny stock. Too many words are a waste. The challenge for the *One Minute Presenter* is to say more with less. This is where taglines come in.

Taglines rule the world. We live in a world of soundbites, slogans and catchphrases. *"Impossible is Nothing"*, *"Imagination at Work"* and *"Connecting People"* are examples of how global brands use taglines to not only promote their products but communicate their values. (See end of this chapter to know the companies these slogans belong to).

You know your happy ending. You have picked your story. Now it's time to tag those key phrases throughout your presentation.

## Taglines are short

People's attention spans are falling. Before mass media like TV came along, public speeches could run for several hours. Today even interviews with top politicians are cut from 13 minutes to 3 minutes – an 80% cut! This is why taglines and slogans are so important.

## WHAT IS A TAGLINE?

Taglines are short catchy marketing phrases which sum up the promise of a brand (or product or movie), and are designed to be memorable and easily passed through a target audience. A good tagline can stand the test of time and become synonymous with a company or product.

The 1975-2005 *"Don't leave home without it"* from American Express and the 1988 *"Just do it"* from Nike taglines show how the power of taglines can carry over into building the world's most valuable brands.

## One word equity

Time is against you when you're presenting. The old adage says you have seconds to make a strong first impression and that still rings true. Can you get your message across before your audience switches off (or more likely switches back to their mobile phones, PDAs and BlackBerrys). Maurice Saatchi, founder of Saatchi and Saatchi, the global advertising firm, is a man who knows a lot about communicating. He coined a phrase *"one word equity"*. This means every successful company "owns a word" which becomes associated with them.

## What word do you own?

Think back to products and companies whose names have become the category. Hoover, Xerox, Vaseline to name a few. More recent examples like Google (search), eBay (online auction) and SKYPE (internet telephony) have all become household names in a few short years. They have even become part of our language with "google it" and "SKYPE me" popping up more in conversation with today's digital natives.

## What is your tagline?

Take a look at your next presentation. Use these steps to form your tagline:

1. Write down your happy ending in 25-50 words.

2. Take a break and come back to this paragraph. Highlight key words or phrases. Now imagine you only had time to deliver one sentence to your audience. Keep the value and meaning of your message. Rewrite it in 10 words or less.

3. Put this aside for several hours or longer. Come back and see which words really sum up the essence of your message. Pick out your key words or phrases.

For The *One Minute Presenter* our nine word tagline is *"succesful business presentations for a short attention span world"*. We use two key phrases: *successful business presentations* and *short attention spans*. The tips in this book are designed to help you in those two areas.

You now have focus in your presentation. This will help you structure your presentation framework. You can check your supporting points, and choice of visuals (charts, graphs, statistics) against your key words. Ask yourself, *"How does this support my key words?"*

With practice, you will be able to quickly get to your key words(s) in a shorter time. It will be a challenge the first few times you try this exercise. Stick with it. You need the focus to capture and engage today's audiences. The clearer your message, the more effective your presentations. Good luck!

## Be aware when you present your ideas

Make your message tangible. Don't make your audience work it out. If you make them think during a presentation, then while they are thinking, they cannot be listening to your subsequent words.

Dr. John Medina, author of *Brain Rules*, vividly demonstrates how the human brain is ill equipped to handle two processing tasks simultaneously. *"Driving while talking on a cell phone is worse*

## WHAT IS YOUR PERSONAL TAGLINE?

A useful exercise for all executives to take is to develop your own personal brand. What slogan sums you up? From my work in building organisations and raising awareness for professional public speaking in China, I was given the moniker: *"The gateway to professional speaking in China"* as I often advise, meet and support international professional speakers whenever they visit China. It clearly states my personal brand position.

How would you like to be known in your organization? What is your tagline? You don't need to publicize it, but at least you will know and this will guide your actions. Become a brand. Tagline yourself!

Avoid jargon, buzzwords and concepts. They confuse and lead to different interpretations. For example, "a quality product" could mean different things to a European sourcing company and his Chinese manufacturing supplier. If you're allowing your audience to interpret the meaning of your message, then you're not doing your job as a presenter delivering of effective communication. Your presentations should have one message and one clear outcome per presentation.

The three slogans were from adidas *(Impossible is Nothing)*, GE *(Imagination at Work)* and Nokia *(Connecting People)*.

*than driving drunk."* This is because the human brain uses something called the attentional spotlight. The attentional spotlight, according to Dr. Medina, cannot multitask which means cellphone-talking car drivers have the same reaction time (when stopping) as a drunk driver.

So don't make your audiences think! Do the thinking for them. Know where you want to take them, shape a clear concept of your overall message, use stories to engage and bite-size your content with slogans, soundbites and taglines. Puzzles are great for long train and plane journeys, but not for successful business presentations.

## Next chapter

The big day is almost here. You have crafted a great message and you know what your audience expects from you. Now it's time to get ready to hold their attention, use some interactive techniques and build up to an engaging presentation. It's time to "Create your Connection".

# – 7 –

# Create your Connection

"Anytime the audience is engaged, it is a success. You can feel it. They respond well and laugh at little things."

*George Stavropoulos, fashion designer, 1920–1990.*

## This chapter's content:

### Three levels to connect with your audience:

## One Minute Learning:

## *Process:*

☞ First, learn the bronze level: **hold attention**.

☞ Second, advance to the silver level: **interact**.

☞ Third, step up to the gold level: **engage.**

# Case study#4:
## *Paul, country manager, specialty chemicals.*

Paul travels throughout Asia and has a challenging role in retaining talent and developing his company's growing Asian business. Despite extensive travel and heavy workload, Paul always prepares thoroughly for a presentation and spends most of his preparation time making slides. During recent presentations, he has noticed his colleagues never seem to be paying attention. They spend a great deal of time holding their mobile phones and BlackBerry devices under the table, messaging and checking their emails. *"It's distracting and I wonder why I bother to prepare for the presentation."* Paul wonders how to get his audience's attention. He is delivering an important message, and wants his audience to hear it.

Sometimes he suddenly gets an idea and moves away from the slides to write on the flip chart, turning his back to the audience. His colleagues have told him this looks rude and unprofessional, but he is not sure how to change this.

He once tried asking questions to an audience in Shanghai, but got no response. He put this down to cultural differences. His CEO recently told Paul that he would be spearheading the roll-out of a new talent management program. He would be expected to do a roadshow across Asia to get buy-in from the team. Paul is worried, as he knows he needs to engage more with his peers.

This chapter provides tools to help you create a better connection with your audience.

The key step in creating a connection with an audience is to build rapport. Rapport is about being able to relate to your audience. When you have rapport, your audience knows you understand them and care about them. When you have rapport, you demonstrate you're able to see the world from the eyes of your audience. There is nothing worse than a speaker who comes out and gives a "canned" presentation - the same presentation he has given 50 times before - without regard for the audience in the room. Look for the five rapport tips in this chapter.

## WHAT IS RAPPORT?

Rapport is a relationship of mutual understanding or trust and agreement between people (2006 Princeton University). Rapport is an essential part of human relationships. Without rapport, we wouldn't have any friends, we wouldn't be able to sell products and we wouldn't enjoy personal relationships.

Rapport has also been called:

- **Chemistry**
- **Trust**
- **Charisma**
- **Empathy**
- **Compatibility**
- **Affinity**

# A. Bronze: Hold Attention

The bronze level for creating a connection is holding the attention of your audience. Once you lose your audience's attention, they're gone. Despite our multitasking approach to work, it really is impossible to be totally focused on two things at the same time.

# Set ground rules

One of the most common interruptions to people's attention is the mobile device attached to every business person. I can't see any way to reverse this trend. It's a fact of business life. As presenters we need to evolve and adapt to this new environment.

You have to address this at the start of your presentation with some ground rules. If you don't tell the audience how to behave in your presentation, you can't complain later when mobile phones disturb your presentation. Here are some ground rules you can use. You can pick and choose and add others:

## GROUND RULES

1. Set start time, break times and finish time.

2. We start on time and finish on time.

3. We'll not go back and review material for those not present at the time.

4. Check emails and messages during breaks, take phone calls outside.

5. Everyone is encouraged to participate.

7. One person talks at a time.

8. Location of rest rooms and emergency exits.

According to John Keller, certain methods are better for grabbing the audience's attention. These include:

**Active participation.**
Adopt strategies such as games, role plays or other hands-on methods to get your audience involved with the material or subject matter

**Variability.**
To better reinforce messages and allow for individual differences in learning styles, use a variety of methods in presenting material (e.g. use videos, short lectures, mini-discussion groups)

**Humor.**
Maintain interest by using a small amount of humor (but not too much to be distracting)

**Specific examples.**
Use an expressive picture, story, or biography

**Inquiry.**
Ask questions or problems for the audience to solve, e.g. brainstorming activities

*Learn more about Keller's motivational design model at www.arcsmodel.com.*

# Writing on flip charts

In our case study, we saw that Paul struggled with flip charts. Most presentations include some kind of visual aid, usually a computer based slideshow or a flip chart. Flip charts can be printed in advance or can be handwritten. One of the quickest ways to break your connection with the audience is to turn your back to them and start writing on a flip chart.

To hold the audience's attention, you need to think through your presentation. Prepare long flip charts in advance. Number them so you know the order and how many sheets you will use. Set up the flip chart so the entire audience can easily view the chart and you do not need to walk across it to change the sheet. Usually a flip chart is placed to the right or left of the presenter.

If you need to write on the flip chart during the presentation to note questions or ideas from the audience, set up another flip chart with a blank sheet ready. Make sure you write from the side of the flip chart, so you can quickly and easily turn to face the audience for their next idea. Or ask for a volunteer writer.

If you commonly use flip charts, you may consider scanning and printing them in high quality large A1 or A0 size so you save time going from presentation to presentation. This is a good idea if you give the same and similar presentations frequently, for example, on a roadshow.

# Sharing yourself

Why do we like spoken presentations? Even in a world of technology, we need human contact. Our storytelling history is so ingrained in our cultures after tens of thousands of years. It's hard to drop the human contact.

You can become a better "storyteller" by showing the audience your human side. This doesn't mean getting really personal and sharing your deep dark secrets (I'm British and it would scare me to do that!). It means showing you're someone just like the people in audience. You share similar hopes, interests, challenges and frustrations, and like the audience, you would like a solution to them. It's common sense that we like to do business with people we like, and it's also backed up by research. Robert Cialdini identified "liking" as one of the key tools of how we are persuaded in his book *Influence*. We only buy from salespeople we like. Joe Girard, once known as the number one car salesman in the world, said his success was due to two factors: a fair price and being likeable. Cialdini's research also found we like people who are similar to us. The more similar we are to someone, the more likely we are to be influential over them. This can include dress, culture, opinions, interests and background. In today's multicultural workplace, we need to get back to human basics to make this connection. So family, education, sports, aspirations and travel can be good ways to show how similar to your audience you are.

If your audience is over forty years old, many will have families and you can share a few quick pictures of your family at the start when you're introducing yourself. With a younger audience, you can mention your love of travel or show pictures of your recent holidays. These personal touches build rapport with your audience and can be used throughout your presentation to catch and hold attention.

## Satisfying audience's curiosity

In any part of the world, there are common questions people ask. By being attentive, you can pick up on these and then turn them into the opening of your presentation, perhaps when you're introducing yourself. It's a good way to connect to the audience. For example, when I present in China, common questions I'm asked include:

- Where are you from?

- How long have you lived in China?

- Why did you come to China?

- Do you speak Chinese?

- Do you like Chinese food?

- Can you use chopsticks?

- Do you like living in Shanghai?

- What's your impression of China?

I weave the answers into my presentations, which keeps the audience's attention and allows them to relate to me beyond my presentation message.

I typically open my presentations in Asia by sharing a quick overview of my life journey from an Irish family in London through my student days in England and finally my travels around the world to Asia and living in Shanghai. I mention my heart is full of Irish passion, my head full of English education and my hands full with having to learn how to use chopsticks! It gets a laugh, breaks the ice and builds rapport. Adding these type of anecdotes into your presentation will keep your audience's attention focused on you.

## RAPPORT TIP#1: EYE CONTACT

Use eye contact to hold attention. Eye contact is the key to maintain rapport. During your presentation, make eye contact with everyone in the audience. If you notice some people are losing concentration, look at them (with a smile) and direct your presentation to them. They will usually re-engage with you and your message.

If two members of the audience start talking, don't take it personally. Look at them (with a smile) and wait for them to stop. Once people see you making eye contact they will usually stop their conversations. As you present, switch your eye contact smoothly to different people. Deliver a few sentences to each person and move on.

# B. Silver: Interact

### How do you interact with your audience?

You're **audience blocked** if you deliver a presentation without any idea of what the audience is doing, thinking, or feeling. You don't see potential interruptions like pen banging or mobile message checking. You don't hear sighs of exhaustion. You don't feel when the audience is lost or doesn't understand your message. In short, you give the same presentation whether the audience is present or not.

You're **audience reliant** when you constantly need the audience's reassurance that you're doing a good job. You're aware of every move from the audience. If one member of the audience looks unhappy, you're willing to stop everything and solve their issues. You're not sure whether you did a good job unless the audience tells you that you're great. In short, the focus is on you, and the audience is there to make you feel better.

You're **audience connected** when you're aware of the feeling in the room. You can see how individual members are reacting and although you don't stop every time you get a negative response (like a yawn or sigh), you do course-correct. You might stop and do a quick recap or ask checking questions. You're aware that the audience only has a limited attention span. You vary the delivery pace, and you insert activities or interactive exercises every 15 or 20 minutes. You share experiences and appropriate stories, and you're willing to have the audience give their input into the presentation. You see the presentation as a shared experience, and actively create the connection with the audience so they give their input. The *One Minute Presenter* is always audience connected.

## Asking simple questions to start

Connecting to the audience is an interactive experience. Connect to the audience as a whole, not only to individuals. Do not *only* focus on those people who encourage you with smiles and head-nods (they are great by the way). Keep your attention on the audience as a whole. Ask simple questions at the beginning of your speech.

### Some can be closed questions:

- Is the traffic always so busy?
- Are you looking forward to learning something?
- Is it always so hot here?

### Others can be more open:

- What did you do over the weekend?
- Where are the good local restaurants?
- Where are the local sights?

The purpose of these questions is not to start an in depth dialog with individuals, but to start audience participation in the presentation. When you see people nodding and smiling, and hear them giving simple answers, you'll know you've connected with the audience and can move into the start of your presentation. Be prepared to answer the questions yourself. For example:

*"Over the weekend I went to see the Bird's Nest Stadium in Beijing. Amazing. Has anyone been there?"*

*"My friend took me to a traditional restaurant. Food was great but I wasn't sure what exactly some of the dishes were!"*

## Link your opening to the location

Always open up with a few comments about the country, city or location where the meeting is being held. If you're in Beijing, you can mention how impressive the Bird's Nest stadium or Water Cube is. Keep your comments positive and respectful of local norms and traditions. If you're presenting to a regular group, you can mention topical news, sports or entertainment topics. Keep it short and upbeat. Your purpose is to break the ice, get people relaxed and "in the room" before you move onto your presentation.

## Creating a hospitable space

Become more interactive by creating a hospitable space so people feel more willing to speak out. Make your meeting room as comfortable as possible. Choose natural light over fluorescent tubes whenever possible. Refreshments should be easy to access with water available at all times. Post up quotes or flip charts which relate to the theme of the presentation. Make sure people have enough space to write notes. Try to get fresh air into the room at breaks. The oxygen will help keep the audience alert!

## RAPPORT TIP#2: SMILE

*Every time you smile at someone, it is an action of love, a gift to that person, a beautiful thing."*

- Mother Teresa.

The influential Greek philosopher Aristotle said, *"Among all animals, only human beings can smile."* A smile is a special gift we give ourselves and we can give to others. One of the most important things in life is to be able to smile. It's free, and everyone can do it. Even when you're in a bad mood, a smile will help you through. Other people judge you on your smile. People who don't smile often are considered serious, fierce and unfriendly. People who smile are judged as pleasant, open and warm. When you smile, people smile back.

## RAPPORT TIP#3: ASK QUESTIONS

To interact and hold an audience's attention you have to be asking questions. Simply asking the question means you're creating a connection with the audience, even if they're not answering them directly. When the brain hears a question it automatically goes to work to evaluate and think about the topic. This is exactly what you want to do. You want your audience to be focused on your topic and message. As we said before, brain research has shown that we can only focus on one thing at a time with excellence.

You can gain attention and build rapport by inserting checking questions or rhetorical questions:

- Do we need to review anything here?
- Does that make sense?
- Is everything clear?
- Is everyone happy here?
- Any question here?
- Can I clarify anything?

Good presenters will use these questions as a transition point in their presentation, and more importantly, look for audience reaction. If your audience is frowning or looking confused, you may need to stop and recap your previous section. If they're smiling and nodding, you can move on.

Don't be afraid if an audience member answers, *"No."* to your *"Is everything clear?"* question. This is a great opportunity for you to focus in on their concern and decide how to resolve it. Feedback is always good. It's much better to get it during the presentation, when you still have a chance to address the concern.

# C. Gold: Engage

### Engaging with the audience

Once you have the audience's attention and have created an environment where you and the audience can interact, you can take a step up the connection podium to *engage* with your audience.

With your deep understanding of who is in your audience, you can now use this knowledge to continually bring the audience closer to you. You know:

- Key "burning issues" on their minds

- Important personalities you need to recognize for their contributions (organizer, boss)

- Who their customers are in detail

- Key vocabulary, buzzwords and phrases

Armed with this information, you can pepper these words and examples throughout your presentation. Use case studies which are relevant to their industry and their target customers. Are they targeting 18 to 24 year old consumers or frequent business travelers? Don't use examples about their competitors. Don't tell Microsoft how great Google is. Small words can make a big difference. Does your audience use "client" instead of "customer"?

This is where your homework before the presentation is essential.

See Chapter 5, "Treasure Your Audience" for detailed techniques on understanding your audience.

A good way to understand these nuances is to have coffee or lunch with someone who knows the audience well. Even a SKYPE call can help you prepare. Continually making these connections will build your credibility with the audience.

If you can't speak to anyone ahead of time, arrive early before your presentation and meet and greet people as they come in. Ask them about their key concerns and what they're looking to learn from this presentation. People are very willing to share if you just ask. You can also use their names during your presentation, which will increase the engagement. For example:

*"Mike was telling me that you just won a big account by using the new approach. This shows some of the benefits a change in perspective can bring to our division."*

## Be enthusiastic

Nothing sells like enthusiasm. The more energetic and excited you are about your topic, the more the audience will buy into you as a credible presenter. Think about the best presenters and salespeople you know. Do they have a twinkle in their eye? How passionate are they about their subject? Enthusiasm doesn't mean you have to be bouncing off the walls with energy or walking on fire in Tony Robbins style. But you do need to be the most passionate person in the room about your topic. Demonstrate your love for learning and improving. Be open to comments and see every challenge as a learning opportunity. If you can convey this energy, your audience will stay engaged with you for longer. Think back to all those droning lecturers you sat through (or slept through) at university, and you'll recall just how important enthusiasm is to effective presenting.

## Be yourself

Review the questions from Chapter 4 and start to add more of your authentic voice into your presentations.

## RAPPORT TIP#4:  USE SELF-DEPRECATING HUMOR

Use humor wisely. I have heard many people suggest the best way to open a presentation is to *"tell a joke"*. This is a high-risk strategy. My advice is never tell a joke to start unless you're a confident joke-teller. There are so many things which can go wrong to blow your credibility out of the water before you even get going. With today's diverse workplaces, it's getting easier to offend someone with an off-color joke.  Here's why:

- Jokes are subjective. Not everyone will find a joke funny

- Even a good joke can be poorly delivered

- Jokes can offend

- Cross-cultural audiences increase risk of unintended offense

Don't get me wrong. I'm not a kill-joy. I love stand-up comedy and host a comedy club night in Shanghai called Chopschticks. The world is a better place for Bill Hicks, George Carlin and Richard Pryor. But in the world of business presentations, jokes are best avoided.

Sometimes it's not even about the joke. One American speaker checked with the organizer about whether it would be fine to use some humor about air travel, as the speaker had just had a tough time getting to the venue. The organizer said it would be better not to, because a year before the company's CEO and CFO lost their lives in a plane crash and it was still on people's minds. The speaker could have totally lost the audience and never known why if he hadn't checked. If you're going to use humor, then don't tell jokes.

I think we get the message. So what can we do to engage with an audience in a light-hearted manner?

I recommend you use self-deprecating humor. Laugh at yourself. Direct the humor towards yourself. For example:

- Challenges you had in a new city

- Surprises you had in a new country

- Your failures (that led to an insight)

- Problems in relationships (that led to a learning point)

- Cultural differences and insight

Whenever you can find stress in an everyday situation, humor follows quickly. In Shanghai, sharing an experience of taking a hair-raising taxi ride or crossing a busy road brings empathic laughter.

Remember: don't go too far. People are coming to listen to you because you're an expert. Don't go in and say, *"I haven't prepared for this, as I'm a terrible presenter!"* That is taking self deprecation too far! Use this type of humor to show your human side, but remember to always retain your credibility.

## RAPPORT TIP#5: USE YOUR BODY

Rapport building uses a lot of non-verbal techniques to increase the trust and connection with the audience. Your body language plays an important role in maintaining connection with your audience. People who are in tune with each other will tend to have similar body language. Just watch a couple walking down the street and you can notice they walk stride for stride with each other. Almost like synchronized swimmers!

When building rapport, you can use a technique called mirroring and matching. For example, face the audience directly without standing behind a lectern.

## Friend or foe

Long before we developed the power of speech, non verbal cues existed. Our ancestors, without language to deliver a message (such as *"are you a friend or a foe?"*), became experts in examining facial gestures and body positions. Small variations in facial expressions could mean literally the difference between life and death. Today non-verbal communication remains an important part of delivering your message. You're always sending a signal with your body language whether you're aware or not.

## Become a body language expert

Become a people watcher. Spend some time in a coffee shop. Look at couples speaking together and see how their body language matches the mood of their conversation.

Guess what kind of relationship they have based on their conversations! This can be fun. Are they:

- Friends
- Co-workers
- Spouses
- Siblings
- Lovers
- First-daters

## WHAT IS MIRRORING AND MATCHING?

When you see two people walking along the street, chatting away and walking stride for stride totally in tandem with each other. You can usually bet these people are good friends. They have rapport. They have a connection.

As humans we like to be in sync with people we care about. Take a look around the next time you're outside and see how in sync people are with each other. Look for couples or groups of young people. This is the concept behind mirroring and matching.

As business people who wish to influence and persuade, we need to be in sync with our audiences in order to better secure their agreement. Mirroring and matching is a technique which can help in small group presentations.

**Guess the topic of the conversation based on their body language:**

- Business partners in agreement or disagreement
- A salesperson pitching a client
- Two friends chatting about football
- Two friends chatting about a cute guy

## Practice with friends

Show how body language is key to rapport building by using negative body language with your friends. You will see the reaction when your body is not in line with your message.

In my workshops, we use an exercise to show how important rapport is while communicating. In small groups, one person leaves the room to prepare a short presentation on a simple topic, like their last holiday. The rest of the group are told, while they're listening, they cannot make eye contact nor match their body language with the presenter. The impact is immediate and immense. I have seen people literally stop their speech in seconds when faced with this audience (of two or three people). We need eye contact as reassurance that we're on the right track. Your body language is very powerful. Use it to connect with your audience. See more rapport tips online at **www.oneminutepresenter.com/rapport**

## Observe professional speakers or salespeople

Watch how expert presenters use their body to connect with the audience. See how they build rapport before they start delivering their messages. Go to YouTube and search for "professional presenters" or "Toastmasters". You can see my YouTube channel by searching for "oneminutepresenter".

# INTERNATIONAL SPEAKING USING ENGLISH TO NON NATIVE AUDIENCES

I have been living and working in Asia since 1994 and at one time was delivering 100 sales presentations a year to high tech firms. I now conduct training and speaking engagements all around Asia and have faced the challenge of presenting to cross cultural audiences.

Language ability is a key concern for every speaker when presenting to a multicultural audience, who are using English as their second language. Many presenters fail to account for differences in language ability when speaking in Asia. They miss opportunities to connect and engage the audience by using language that is not understood.

Change and adjust your speaking style to match the audience. The audience won't be able to adapt to your style quickly enough. Make their life easier. Using appropriate language will keep you connected with the audience. This allows you to deliver your informative and entertaining message, which will benefit the lives of the audience.

I have personally slowed down my speaking pace, made sure my pronunciation is clear and reduced the complexity of my language when speaking to diverse groups internationally. This means no slang, idioms, acronyms or complex vocabulary. Simple, plain language always works well.

## Next chapter

On your journey as a *One Minute Presenter*, you will work on improving your vocal power and use subtle ways to project credibility to your audience. Prepare to "Deliver with Style".

# – 8 –

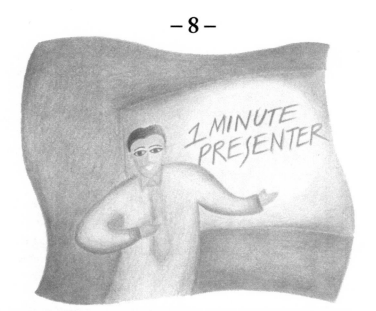

## THE FIFTH STATION:

# Deliver with Style

"Practice as if you are the worst. Perform as if you are the best."

*Anon.*

## This chapter's content:

### Build up your voice with five essential skills:

▶ A. Volume.
*Page 99*

▶ B. Speed or rate.
*Page 103*

▶ C. Pitch or tone.
*Page 106*

▶ D. Emphasis.
*Page 108*

▶ E. Pause.
*Page 110*

### Cultivate five key non-verbal skills:

▶ A. Eye contact.
*Page 112*

▶ B. Postures.
*Page 115*

▶ C. Gestures.
*Page 116*

▶ D. Body movement.
*Page 121*

▶ E. Face.
*Page 123*

### Slideshow presentations
*See page 125*

## One Minute Learning:

● 13 essential tips to use your voice powerfully
*Page 96-111*

● Maximize your message with 11 non verbal tips
*Page 112-124*

● The dos and don'ts of slideshow presenting
*Page 125-132*

## Process:

☞ First, scan the tips and pick out any areas you need to work on urgently.

☞ Second, make a plan to start building up your delivering skills over time.

☞ Third, read this chapter again before a presentation and put a tip to the test.

# Case study#5:
## J.S. Chen, finance director, semiconductors.

J.S. has been working for his company for a long time now. He has good technical knowledge and his technical experience is very strong. He works long hours and is regarded as being very committed to finish his projects completely and on time. A year ago, J.S. noticed his managers began to ignore him more and more when it came to delivering presentations inside the department and at outside conferences. J.S. asked himself on more than a few occasions, *"How can they choose other less talented people to take the spotlight?"*

At that time, J.S. wanted to find a way to express his experience and knowledge with more conviction. However, he was known for his soft voice, which did not project well when speaking in public. He knew his message well but found it difficult to deliver it dynamically to the audience. He was not sure how to increase his voice power and body language.

Through a friend's recommendation, J.S. came across a systematic program which worked through the components of vocal power and how body language is connected to the spoken message. He tried some of the techniques and became more active during smaller internal meetings. As his confidence grew, he took the initiative to speak at industry forums and round tables. He became known for being a willing presenter and as his skills improved, so did his confidence. He found a style which worked for him. Today, he is regarded as *the* expert in his industry, and is frequently invited to conferences.

This chapter gives a comprehensive look into the mechanics of how to improve your delivery.

# Build Up Your Voice With Five Essential Skills

Your voice is your main weapon in your presenting arsenal. A good vocal variety will hold the audience's attention much longer than a monotone dull delivery.

## Why is the voice important in a presentation?

The voice can make the difference between a dry, boring presentation and one full of energy, purpose and direction. Your voice is a key factor in conveying everything from complex concepts to adding emotion and sincerity.

## How your voice adds value

Variety is the spice of life. Vocal variety is how you add spice to your presentations. Everyone has different vocal volume, speed and pitch, so how you vary your voice will add impact. While imitating professionals can help you develop certain skills, you will find your speaking voice through practice and self-awareness. Top speakers with excellent vocal power include Barack Obama and Bill Clinton (US politicans); Zig Ziglar and Anthony Robbins (motivational speakers); Joel Osteen and Rick Warren (pastors).

Before we get into analyzing your voice, let's refresh some basic tips.

## Tip 1: Record every speech you deliver

Listen to yourself on a tape or MP3 recorder. It's an experience you will never forget. The first time I heard myself on a recording, I asked myself, *"Who is that speaking?"* followed by extreme embarrassment! With persistence, I realized my vocal strengths and weaknesses and worked on them.

# WHY DOES MY VOICE SOUND DIFFERENT ON A TAPE RECORDER/ MICROPHONE?

**Dr. Chris Smith of The Naked Scientist**

There's nothing worse than hearing a recording of your voice for the first time! The reason is that how we think we sound isn't really how we sound. Inside your ears there is an organ called a cochlea: a special neurological structure that converts the vibrations of sounds in the air into electrical signals that the brain can understand. It gets stimulated by the pressure waves caused by sounds in the air, but at the same time can pick up the vibration of the bones in your skull. When you're listening to sounds in the environment, the chief source of those sounds is coming through the air, very little comes through the bone. When you're speaking, however, your whole head resonates; it vibrates. This means that your cochlea gets stimulated by your skull vibrating, as well as the sound coming out of your mouth and going through the air to your ears. The body does two things: it gets a different version of those vibrations (through the bone and the ear), but it also has a protective mechanism to cut down the amount of sound which is going into the cochlea. It reduces sensitivity of your ear a little when you're speaking, so you get a slightly different rendition of what your voice sounds like. That's why, when you hear yourself recorded and played back, you sound totally different, because all you hear back from the tape recorder is sound coming through the air, minus the skull vibration and bone conduction.

*Reprinted with permission from*
*www.thenakedscientists.com*

## WHAT VOICE RECORDER SHOULD I USE?

Today buying a good quality voice recorder is very affordable and many can record to MP3 file formats, which can then be easily transferred and played on your computer. I use a Sanyo digital recorder which cost around USD100. There are many other similar products available.

I also discovered my phone has an excellent one touch voice recorder, check out the HTC smartphone range.

I would recommend you research and compare models on Cnet (www.cnet.com) and then shop locally if you live outside North America.

# Tip 2: Use a microphone at every opportunity

Professional speakers use microphones all the time. It's better to be heard and understood, than not to be. It's not a contest. Be effective. Use a microphone. The size of audience is a factor as well. If the audience is over 40 people, use a microphone.

You can use :

| Types of Microphone | Description | Occasions to Use |
|---|---|---|
| Fixed microphone | Attached to a lectern or on a stand. | Formal occasions. A host or MC will often introduce speakers from a lectern. |
| Wired microphone | Clipped onto a stand with a boom arm and long wire to allow movement. | When a wireless microphone is not available and you need to move around the stage. |
| Wireless microphone | Hand-held microphone. | Most commonly used as it allows easy movement across the stage. |
| Clip on microphone (also called lapel or lavaliere ) | Small microphone is attached to your clothing, often comes with battery pack to attach to your belt or slip into inside pocket of jacket. | If the venue has one, use it. It frees your hand, allowing you to gesture and move freely on the stage. |
| Ear microphone | Clipped around ear sometimes with headset. | In public, think big motivational speakers, like Antony Robbins. Use only if you have a big personality. Often used for TV interviews and recording teleseminars and podcasts. |

We'll now break the voice into its components so we can improve each aspect and build a good quality voice to increase engagement and connection with your audience:

A. Volume.

B. Speed or rate.

C. Pitch or tone.

D. Emphasis.

E. Pause.

# A. Volume

What kind of music do you like to listen to? Are you a fan of hip-hop like swim legend Michael Phelps or is Vivaldi more your thing? The volume you listen to your music affects your mood. That's why heavy metal music has to be played full blast no matter what the situation and love ballads from Barry White tend to work best when played as background music.

Your voice in a presentation greatly impacts the mood of your audience. Low gentle voices will put the audience to sleep. Loud bellowing voices will make you look like you had too much coffee or Red Bull. The key is variety and linking this variety to your message and the mood you wish to convey to your audience.

## The volume scale

Using your vocal variety is the key to holding attention over your audience. Throughout your speech you can raise and lower volume to add impact to your message.

On a scale of 0 to 10, judge your speaking volume. Let's assume "5" is your normal speaking volume. So this would be a volume you would use if you were speaking to a friend or a team member.

## What effect does volume have on your audience?

| Volume | Impact on Speech |
| --- | --- |
| 10 | Grabs attention |
| 9 | Creates excitement |
| 8 | Builds up a climax |
| 7 | |
| 6 | Normal speaking range |
| 5 | Conversational style |
| 4 | |
| 3 | Brings audience towards you |
|  | Creates tension |
| 2 | Shows sincerity |
|  | Expresses the seriousness of a topic |
| 1 | Whisper |
| 0 | Silence or a "pause" |

## The volume scale ranges

### Loud (8-10)

**When to use:** Add emphasis on key message. Build up to a climax.

10 – Shouting at the top of your voice (not advised for presentations. Save for sporting events and music concerts!)

9 – Large groups only; adds energy

8 – Groups under 20; adds energy

### Normal (4-7)

**When to use:** This is your "default" volume. Should take a conversational style, which is adequate for the audience to hear but not overpowering.

### Quiet (1-3)

**When to use:** Attracts attention. Creates suspense and emotion.

## Tip 3: Start with energy

Openings are important and you should start at a "7" or "8". The first 30 seconds should be full of energy and raising your volume is a good way to :

- Catch attention

- Direct focus on you

- Sound confident

- Make sure your opening message is clearly heard

## Tip 4: Increase your volume when making a transition

For example, you can say at a volume of "7", *"Now as we move onto the second section..."* This will help your audience understand you're ready to move forward. It's a signal that will help the audience stay with you.

# HOW CAN PEOPLE WITH LOW VOICES SPEAK LOUDER?

Increase your volume, and your speaking confidence will follow. First, record your voice so you're aware of how you sound when you speak. After listening, ask yourself, *"Does this sound like a low voice?"* Could your audience follow you? Then, you can start to work on parts of your speech to increase the volume. At the start of a speech aim to say the first few phrases at a higher volume. Conclude a speech on a higher volume as well.

See the table below on how your volume will change depending on how close you are speaking to somebody. Imagine you are talking across a room or to somebody at the back of a meeting room. Your volume will increase as you need to project more to be heard.

| Distance Between Faces | Tone of Voice | Type of Message |
|---|---|---|
| very close (5-15 cm) | soft whisper | top secret or sensual |
| close (10 -30 cm) | audible whisper | very confidential |
| neutral (50 cm - 1 m) | soft voice, low volume | personal subject matter |
| neutral (1.5 m) | full voice | non-personal information |
| across the room (3-6 m) | loud voice | talking to a group |
| stretching the limits (6-7 m indoors and up to 30 m outdoors) | loud hailing voice | departures and arrivals |

Derived from The Silent Language by Edward Hall (1959)

# B. Speed or rate

When I was in Arizona, I went to see the Grand Canyon, which is awesome. I took a vintage locomotive train to arrive at the Canyon (catch from Williams **www.thetrain.com**). It's a great way to enjoy the beautiful environment and imagine what travel was like 100 years ago. For a holiday it was perfect and especially when you have as wonderful a host like Raleigh Pinskey (**www.promoteyourself.com**). But whenever I'm on my way to the airport in Pudong, Shanghai, the only way to travel is on the maglev – a train glides along on a magnetic field at speeds of up to 431 km/h. As a business traveler, eight minutes to the airport suits me fine.

The speed of your transportation vehicle impacts your mood. The steam train makes you feel relaxed, while the maglev arouses energy. Likewise your vocal speed also impacts how your message affects your audience.

## Speed, pace or rate

Just as the volume of your voice must be appropriate for your audience, the pace or rate at which you speak should be particular to the material or the substance of your speech. Dr. Candice Coleman reminds us that *"serious content is going to be paced more slowly than that which is light and up-beat. Be careful not to let yourself get too fast or you'll stumble and get sloppy. You'll also 'wear out' your audience."*

Have you ever seen a presentation when the speaker rushes through his lines? It's easy to miss much of what he was saying, simply because he didn't take the time to slow down and vary his pace. I've found as an audience member when I don't understand what a speaker is saying, I begin to wonder if the speaker himself knows! So if you tend to get nervous and rush through a presentation, in the eyes of your audience, your credibility drops.

# What effect does speed have on your audience?

| Speed | Effect on Audience |
|---|---|
| Very fast | Use rarely and never because you're running out of time! |
| Fast | Use in bursts. Adds energy, shows passion. |
| Normal | Your normal speaking in public. |
| Slow | Emphasis. Use to repeat a question before answering. More serious content. |
| Very slow | Use only when introducing a new acronym, brand name or a difficult-to-pronounce word. |

## Tip 5: Speed and content go together

To see how important rate is to the message, try this simple exercise. Pick up a newspaper and read a story at a speed which is inappropriate for the content. For example, read a fashion story or sports item very very slowly. Read a political piece very fast. You will soon feel that pace is a very important part of your message delivery. Use your change of rate to add emphasis to your message.

## Tip 6 : Measure your speaking speed

Remember that the speed you speak aloud in a formal speech will be different to your reading speed or even your rate when speaking to friends. Test your speed by reading the following passage and timing how long it takes:

*Obstacles to effective coaching include time and workload pressures. Busy executives will push this relationship down the priority list when faced with other operational pressures. Some companies write succession planning into expatriate contracts. Terms include the selecting and grooming of a successor. Companies would be advised to write these terms into all executive level contracts for all staff. Putting succession planning as a KPI would help spread know-how to future leaders in a more structured way. All good relationships are built on good chemistry. While this is hard to measure, some tools do exist to help match mentor and talent.*

Time in seconds: _____

Divide by 60, then multiply by 100: _____

This is your speaking rate in words per minute.

## Tip 7: Calculate your speech length

If you use a script, simply see how many words you have in your script. In your word processing software, go to tools> word count. Then divide by your speaking rate per minute. You can get an estimate for the amount of time you will speak without interruption. So if your rate is 140 words per minute and your script length is 1000 words, you would expect your speech to take just over 7 minutes. If you expect interaction from the audience or long pauses in parts of your speech, you can add this time to your speech time to estimate the length of your presentation.

# C. Pitch or tone

Not golf or baseball pitches, but musical pitch. I was brought up in a catholic boys school and we went to church twice a week. The church choir would blast out a few merry tunes and we would be off outside to play football. Every choir is divided up into four types of singer: soprano, alto, tenor and bass. A soprano or treble sings in the highest vocal range (think Aled Jones circa 1982 or Dame Kiri Te Kanawa), down the scale to a tenor (like Luciano Pavarotti) and finally a bass singing in the lowest vocal range (think Figaro in The Marriage of Figaro).

While we don't expect you to sing your presentations (although that would be memorable, wouldn't it?), your pitch or tone can be used when you need to add feeling to your speech. Generally, women have a higher pitch and men have a lower pitch. But remember that it's how you vary your tone that will add the impact.

### What effect does varying pitch have on your audience?

| Pitch | Effect on Audience |
|---|---|
| Very high | Use rarely as your voice will sound stretched and out of control. |
| High | Adds excitement and enthusiasm. |
| Normal | Your normal pitch. |
| Low | Shows sincerity. |
| Very low | Serious. |

Pitch changes are used together with volume and speed changes. Slower parts of your speech are often matched with a lower tone. If you're feeling nervous, you can "pitch up", which drives that excess energy into your voice and turns the nerves into enthusiasm. Remember that variety is always the key to a pleasant speaking voice. A constant pitch can convey negative emotions. For example, a constant high could come across as very nervous, while a continual low pitch shows tiredness and boredom.

## Changing your pitch

### Tip 8: Listen to TV news

While listening to the news, listen out for the changes in pitch as the newscaster reads the news. For serious headline stories, listen out for a lower tone that indicates the serious nature of the content. For light hearted items, or for sports, listen out for a higher tone which delivers energy and enthusiasm.

**Talkshows.** See how during a talkshow, the host changes pitch according to the seriousness of a topic (see how Oprah does it).

**Political speeches.** Observe how politicans change their tone according to the emotion they wish their audience to feel. See the excerpt below from a political speech. As the speaker got to the word "fundamentally", his pitch started to go higher and increased throughout the rest of the soundbite. This helped emphasise his message of "change in America." This increase in pitch was also accompanied by an increase in volume. Here is the excerpt:

*We are ready to take this country in a fundamentally new direction. That's what's happening in American right now. Change is what's happening in America.* - Barack Obama, New Hampshire primaries, 2008.

## Tip 9: Match your pitch to emotions you want to convey

Using what you have learned about pitch, you can now think about parts of your speech where you want to let the audience feel, for example, motivated (use higher pitch). Change your pitch and the audience will follow your mood more closely.

Think about how you could convey:

- Enthusiasm

- Passion

- Surprise

- Shock

- Conviction

From what you have learned in the previous tips, think about how you will combine volume, speed and pitch to have the greatest impact on the audience. Try adding them into your next presentation.

# D. Emphasis

Emphasis is a useful voice tool that can bring attention to certain parts of your presentation. Words can be given a heavier emphasis when you want to reinforce a key word. Emphasis is the spoken equivalent of using the "**Bold**" or "underline" function when writing. Putting an emphasis or accent on certain words will:

- Highlight key messages

- Bring out a certain word that is essential

- Help the audience to understand which part is important in your presentation

## Tip 10: How emphasis changes meaning

Let's see how putting emphasis on different words in a sentence will change its meaning:

"*Today* we'll be covering three main topics."

The above sentence places emphasis on "today." This could have been in reply to a "when" question. Or the presenter may just wish to bring this to the audience's attention. Emphasis could be placed on a different word:

"Today we'll be covering *three* main topics."

Now the emphasis is on "three". This could be answering a "how many" question. Or the presenter could want to let the audience know the number of topics covered. You can try this by putting the emphasis on other words, like "*we*" or "*main*".

## Tip 11: Add emphasis into your speech

Listen back to a recording of one of your presentations (you're recording them, right?). What words are you putting emphasis on? Are these the key words? Many speakers will over emphasize irrelevant words. Make sure that you're only accenting those words which are related to your message. Take a look through your presentation script or slides. Find ways that you can add extra emphasis to certain words and phrases (like your sound bites) so the audience's attention is brought to these key words and messages.

# E. Pause

I like to think of the pause as using "the power of silence". The difference between a top professional speaker and a fresh presenter is the ability to be comfortable with silence. Nervous speakers need to fill every single second with a sound, even if the words are not connected with the message. Rambling away from the main topic and adding filling sounds like "er, um, ah" come into the speech. A professional presenter uses the pause.

## Benefits of pausing:

- Allows audience to reflect on a key message

- Indicates that an important point is about to come

- Gives speaker time to think (even professionals can lose their place for a second)

- Separates main sections in a presentation

## The impact it has on the audience:

- Builds trust as the speaker radiates confidence

- Allows a small space for reflection

- Gets the audience's attention back on the speaker

Listen to good presenters and observe how they use the pause in their speeches.

## Tip 12: Use a pause before and after your key messages

A pause signals that you have just said something of importance. It adds impact. Here is how you can use the pause:

### 1. Pause before

To refocus the audience's attention on you. This also builds up the tension and the audience will ask themselves, "What's coming next?"

### 2. Deliver your message

Make sure it's well paced, loud and clear.

### 3. Pause after

To allow the audience to think about the important sentence. It often requires a second or two for the audience to catch up with what you have just said. Remember that this is the first time that they have heard you say it.

To see the pause in good effect, observe a stand up comedian. Once a punch line has been delivered, the comedian waits for the audience to laugh. If he moved straight onto his next joke, the punchline would be wasted as the audience would start listening to the next joke without really absorbing the previous joke. Be brave. Deliver your message. Count to three (one, two, three). Then move on.

## Tip 13: How often to use the pause

Don't use too often. Use once per section (7 to 10 minutes of speaking). Look through your content and identify your key messages, or key phrases. Try and add a pause when you're delivering. Your confidence and poise will shine through.

# Cultivate Five Key Non-Verbal Skills

Non-verbal connection covers all the ways to add impact to your message without speaking. This includes:

A. Eye contact.

B. Posture.

C. Gestures.

D. Body movement.

E. Face.

# A. Eye Contact

Eye contact has played a very important part of human evolution. Making eye contact signals a range of emotions, from love to fear and anger. People make eye contact in different ways depending on their status and familiarity.

Basically, eye contact signals the message that *"all my actions from now on are for you and for you only, others can ignore these signals"* according to Dr. Desmond Morris' research in body language. So your eyes are the most powerful way to connect with and keep connection with your audience. You need to remember that unless you scan your entire audience and give them eye contact, you're going to lose the audience's attention. You have to give everybody eye contact.

In the West, looking people in the eye is a sign of honesty and confidence. Steady and direct eye contact will convey these key benefits to your audience:

- Show sincerity

- Display confidence

- Engage your audience

## Why eye contact connects you with your audience

At its basic level, communication is an interaction between two "people"- the speaker, and the audience. As speakers, it's our responsibility to make sure our message gets to the audience. To do this effectively, it's important to engage the audience. In other words to create an environment where the audience is focused on you and your message.

As a presenter, your purpose is to take your audience to a place where you can positively influence them with your message. If the message does not get across to the audience, you cannot reach your purpose. Using eye contact is a powerful way to establish a connection with your audience so that you can engage them with your message.

Primates, like monkeys and apes, use eye contact as a way to start or avoid interactions. So if we take this forward, by using eye contact we can build better interactions or connections with our audience. Without eye contact we are avoiding our audience. This will lower rapport and reduce your chances of success as a speaker.

## WHY DO WE NEED TO KEEP THE AUDIENCE ENGAGED?

Most people today are overwhelmed with information. People have so many things running through their minds. In a meeting situation, minds wander after 7 or 8 minutes. Mobile phone messaging and mobile devices, like BlackBerrys and PDAs, are constantly being scanned and messages tapped into them. People suffer from CPA - continuous partial attention.

Today, as the pace of society increases, with the spread of internet based services (online banking, shopping, etc.), the number of interactions we have with computers is increasing while personal interactions with people are falling. It's common for people to spend a whole day without making eye contact with another human. Communicating electronically by email, messaging services (MSN) and using SKYPE increases this barrier. People need to feel respected. Have you ever felt respected when talking to someone who wasn't making eye contact? It's impossible. We need eye contact to feel that we are being listened to. We need eye contact to establish rapport, and we need eye contact to establish and maintain a connection with another person. For speakers competing with a range of distractions, eye contact can become a tool to make connections with the audience and to hold their attention.

## Tip 14: Culture and eye contact

Traditionally the eyes have played an important part in many ancient cultures with the famous quotation *"the eyes are the window of the soul"* first mentioned in the Bible.

Studies by Burgoon on how different cultures react to eye contact show that in Japan, listeners are taught to focus on a speaker's neck in order to avoid eye contact. While in the U.S., listeners are encouraged to gaze into a speaker's eyes. Be aware of the cultural background of your audience and adjust the amount of time you spend making eye contact accordingly. Reduce your gaze to 2 or 3 seconds with Asian cultures and extend a little longer with Western cultures. The intensity of your gaze can also make an impact. Avoid really deep stares. Save this for your loved ones, as you may make the audience feel uncomfortable or intimidated.

## Tip 15: Make a connection with your audience

While making eye contact, speak directly to the person as though they are the only person in the audience. When the person smiles or nods, you know your connection has been made. The more connections you can make with the audience throughout your speech, the more successful you will be in engaging the audience.

# B. Postures

Good posture is balance. Think of a soldier standing on sentry duty. Feet firmly on the ground. Back straight. Stomach in. Shoulders back. Eyes looking straight forward. Now relax a little. Most good presenters and confident speakers do have an upright and straight posture. Hands are held above waist level and not crossed. The reasons why we associate an upright posture with success goes back to our animal roots.

Submissive behaviour is linked to making your body appear small. So when attacked, a submissive individual will hunch his shoulders and bend his body so that the aggressor will win and back off. If you see somebody walking down the street with rounded shoulders and a neck hanging forward you will assume that something bad has happened to them. In Asian culture, the bow, kowtow or salaam all have roots in wishing to appear smaller than the other. We use words like 'a big shot' to mean a successful person. 'Standing ten feet tall' means feeling extremely confident. So over time, size and height has come to be connected with dominant status. Project confidence by standing tall and erect while presenting.

If you spend hours in front of a computer, chances are your posture needs improving. Have you ever seen how some people sit at a computer? Arched spine, shoulders rolled forward and stretched necks. Not a pretty sight! And terrible for our posture. A simple way to think of good posture is either you're standing tall or you're becoming a ball. Standing tall with a straight back is attractive. It projects confidence and good health. Look around at people, who are projecting that confidence. They are probably not all hunched up (like a ball) with a curved spine. My mum used to tell me when I was a young boy that I should stand up straight. And now I know why: she wanted me to become a good presenter later in life!

### Tip 16: Good posture starts with breathing

Breathing deep from your stomach helps your back remain straight. There are many good books that show this connection, and the boom in yoga is helping more people reap the benefits of good posture. You could also use the Alexander Technique to release tight posture in the head, neck and shoulders. See **www.alexandertechnique.com**. Look around for examples of good posture in athletes, politicians, and military personnel.

### Tip 17: Use exercise to promote good posture

Regular exercise such as walking, swimming, or bicycling will help the body stay aerobically fit and improve posture.

### Tip 18: Sitting straight

Keep a straight back while sitting by using a high backed chair. Sit with your hips as far back as you can. Look around at some of the ergonomically designed chairs, like the Zody System 89 from Haworth (www.haworth.com).

The next time you walk into a presentation, you will be standing tall and ready to project the right image to the audience: confidence and credibility.

# C. Gestures

Dr. Desmond Morris defines a gesture as *"any action that sends a visual signal to an onlooker."* From ancient history, gestures had powerful meanings attached to them. Take a simple gesture like the "thumbs-up", which in many countries means good or great. This came from the blood sport arenas of Ancient Rome. For entertainment two gladiators would fight to the death (a bit like today's Mixed Martial Arts fighting!). When a fight was especially bloody and crowd pleasing, the crowd would give a thumbs-up or a thumbs-down. The thumbs-up expressed that the loser could keep his life. The thumbs-down, the loser dies. If enough of the crowd gave the thumbs-up, the emperor might decide to give the final verdict of a thumbs-up to spare the loser. Even then the rulers knew how to please the masses without market surveys and focus groups!

Rome was a very public and ritualistic society and from this many gestures were derived. Likewise, in China during the Qing Dynasty, when men of the same social status met each other, they used certain gestures. When meeting with the emperor, a very strict format of gestures was used. Unlike the populism of Rome, these gestures were confined to the ruling classes, so when the Dynasty passed on so did the gestures. Gestures changed with the times.

The main reason to use gestures is the added emphasis that they can bring to your message when coordinated with your spoken message. In the examples above, the gestures are fixed in a certain context, so that the meaning is 100% clear. In today's world of business presentations, we do not have such a fixed context for our gestures (except some very rude ones!).

Think of the classic "OK" sign that an American might make by making a circle with his thumb and forefinger. This can only mean one thing to him that everything is good. But in different cultures this same gesture can mean drastically different things. In Japan, it's the gesture for money. In France, it means worthless. In Greece, it's an insult.

Compare this to the naval world, where semaphore is used to communicate via the position of flags. Or at a horse racing track where tic-tac is used to communicate the changing betting odds before a race starts. The gestures are very clear in the context. Everybody using them understands their meaning. As business presenters we need to learn the basic gestures and the messages they convey.

I'm going to focus on the movements made by your hands and arms. When presenting there are a couple of gestures to generally avoid:

## 1. Closed gestures

Crossed arms, folded arms or wrapping arms across your body conveys resistance, rejection or self protection. This closed gesture has its root in our ancient culture when wrapping your arms around yourself was used to avoid attack and to signal to your attacker that you were submissive and not a threat to them.

## 2. Touching nose and covering mouth

Conveys uncertainty and nervousness. The nose touch is often connected to deception and covering up a lie for two reasons. Firstly, it's a disguised attempt to cover the mouth. When a person is lying they subconsciously cover their mouth to stop themselves. You can observe this in little children and it explains why your mother told you not to speak with your hand over your mouth! The second reason is the physiological reaction to lying. When a person lies they initially have a fear of being caught in the lie. This leads to the blood circulations draining from the face. However, as they sit and continue with the lie, blood flows back into the face - sometimes seen as blushing in children – and into the tissues of the nose. This results in a tingling feeling that results in a quick touch from the hand. Popular children's book *Pinocchio* symbolized this reaction because whenever the puppet told a lie his nose grew longer and longer!

Dr. Alan Hirsch of the Smell and Taste Treatment and Research Foundation in Chicago, and Dr. Charles Wolf of the University of Utah, made a detailed analysis of Bill Clinton's grand jury testimony in August 1998, when the President denied having had sex with Monica Lewinsky. They discovered that while Clinton was telling the truth he hardly touched his nose at all, but that when he lied about the affair, he touched his nose once every four minutes on average for a grand total of 26 times. So it's not a good idea to touch your nose during your presentations. Your audience may think that you are lying!

# Tip 19: Start by using some simple gestures

Remember that the key to adding impact with gestures is the coordination of gestures with your spoken message.

**Try these simple gestures for:**

- Firstly, secondly, thirdly.

- Increasing

- Volatile

- Staying the same

- Exactly (or precisely)

Use gestures-key word combinations to make your messages more vivid and memorable.

# Tip 20: Coordinating gestures with speech

A music conductor uses his gestures to beat out time for the orchestra to follow. Similarly, a presenter uses gestures to emphasize key words to the audience. An enthusiastic presenter may be continually gesturing in an excited attempt to convey his speech. When this becomes too distracting, gestures do not add impact to your message. Instead, it becomes confusing for the audience because they're not sure what exactly it is you want to emphasize.

A presenter to a large audience may use exaggerated gestures so that the audience can follow. Beware of over-exaggerated gestures as these convey insincerity. For example, when two men are play fighting, they use over exaggerated movements to signal that the fight is not real. The more you exaggerate your gestures the more the audience thinks of slap stick humour, like the Marx Brothers, The Three Stooges and Hong Kong movies. Try this out in your rehearsals:

1. Look in a mirror.

2. Video yourself.

3. Ask yourself: What is my message here? Does my gesture add impact to my speech? This will help you coordinate your spoken words with your gestures.

## Tip 21: Make up your own gestures

Added impact comes when your gestures are in tune with your speech. To convey preciseness you will tend to touch the tips of your fingers with your thumb. If you're talking about power or strength, you will use your whole hand, tight fist or chop or punch into your palm.

Make a list of words of that you commonly use during your presentations. How can you convey these words purely through body language? There is more than one right answer here. How would you gesture these words:

- Strategy (think "big picture")
- Integration
- Connecting

How could you turn your key messages into a gesture? Start becoming more aware of how other people use their gestures. Have fun with it. You are a people watcher now!

# D. Body Movement

Moving during a presentation is a good way to stay engaged with an audience. We all remember the long school and university lectures we received with the professor anchored behind the lectern for an hour or two. But we can't remember what he was saying! We just remember it was dull. Moving can help you increase the energy of your delivery and, when used well, help the audience break up your speech into its different sections.

Work your platform. Although in a corporate setting you may only have a small stage to work with, you can still use this to your advantage. You can position yourself nearer the audience when you would like to connect with them on a key point, or to open up with a personal story. You can switch positions on the stage as you explain different key points. This helps the audience separate your main ideas.

## Tip 22: Be aware of your movement

Keep your weight evenly balanced. Nervous speakers shift their weight from one foot to the other, which leads to a bouncing effect when done repetitively. Avoid the "caged tiger" movement of pacing up and down the room like a captive animal. It doesn't project the right image! Other distracting movements to avoid:

- Jiggling coins (or imaginary coins) in your pocket
- Digging both hands deeply in your pockets
- Holding onto your belt
- Playing with your glasses
- Adjusting your clothes
- Playing with your hair

## Tip 23: Use three key questions to improve body movement and gestures

Be yourself. While it's good to observe experts and wonderful speakers to pick up tips and techniques, always remember: never try to imitate other speakers as your performance will appear unnatural and forced. Be yourself. Instead use these three questions that every top speaker uses in evaluating their body movements.

### Is it natural?

A top presenter is like a dancer in the sense that their body moves are in the flow. They are graceful, powerful and confident. Every dancer has a different style. So will you as you develop your speaking style. Observe from the best. Use what works for you.

### Is it under control?

You're using your non verbal communication at a conscious level. You know what you're doing and how it's adding impact to your speech. You have planned how you will move during your speech.

### Is it precise?

Your movement should be in tune with your spoken message. Have you thought about how you can add impact to your message through adding movement and gestures?

## Tip 24: Coordinate body movement with speech outline

Think about how you can move from one part of the stage (or room) to deliver your first section, then move to another part of the room for your second section. By physically moving as you're transitioning onto a new topic, you will help the audience follow along with your message.

By successfully adding body movement into your presentation, you're taking your delivery in a new and higher level.

# E. Face

Making a good connection with your face is easy. Just smile. Especially if - like me- you have a serious face. I was told by my first boss that I should smile more around the office. I'm still working on it! Practice your smile. Use a mirror and find a smile that works for you. As babies and children have known for thousands of years, a smile is the best way to break the ice.

It's not a good idea to try to deliver your entire speech with a forced smile on your face! In most cultures you would appear, well, crazy. Good times to smile are at the beginning of your presentation while you're welcoming, thanking and introducing your speech. You can also use your smile as a transition from one main idea to another if it fits with your message. Also, you should note that in Asian cultures people do like to see smiling faces more than in the West.

All non-verbal communication should match with your spoken message. Serious topics or serious points, for example, talking about issues that may affect people's lives negatively, may not be the best time to smile. Other facial expressions are used less often in formal presentations, so be aware of these often unconscious facial movements.

## Raising eyebrows

Most cultures perform a very rapid eyebrow-raising action during greeting. So you can use this when you get a tough or unfair question or comment directed at you. Avoid overuse as it makes you seem uncertain or unprepared. A

## WHY SMILE?

A smile is a meta-signal, which Dr. Desmond Morris defines as "a signal about signals". Generally a smile indicates that everything is all right. So if you noticed two men fighting, but with smiles on their faces, you would assume that it was just a play fight. Similarly, if you smile at a friend before teasing them about something, they will know that you're being light hearted about the subject. A smile means "everything is good."

longer eyebrow raise means either genuine or mock surprise.

## Winking

Meaning playfulness. Can be used once if it fits with your speaking style. Can also be seen as flirting, so may not be appropriate in some corporate settings.

## Blinking

Meaning surprise or often an unconscious tick.

## Protruding tongue, lip licking

When used unconsciously can signal annoyance. Also, often used in flirting so best avoided.

## Pouting lips

Best left for social settings only!

# Slideshow Presentations

Most "Death by PowerPoint" sessions create audience massacres because they forget that the focal point should be the audience, not the slides. Interaction is one of the best ways to prevent an over-reliance on slides. See Chapter 7 on "Create your Connection".

## Big "No Nos" for slides:

- Reading the words off a slide (you don't do this right? Please say you don't!)

- Slides are packed full of text and complex charts

- Repetitive sound effects, whizzy animations and slide transitions

- Are used as a memory prompt for speaker, not for audience

- Music added to transitions so that every time you click forward to another slide, a sound effect blasts out

- While we are on transitions, let's cut out the crazy transitions. Pick one or two transition styles and stick with it for the presentations

## Slides should:

- Highlight key points

- Clarify your ideas

- Summarize key messages

- Use the familiar acronym Keep It Short and Simple (KISS)

- Use illustrative pictures that tell a story

Technology failures are inevitable. You must be prepared to deliver a presentation without slides. This will reduce your anxiety greatly. Ask yourself this powerful question before each presentation: *"If the power went off in the middle of this presentation, could I continue and still have the same effect on my audience?"*

Your slides are not your presentation! The content of your slides supports your key messages using pictures, charts, videos and bullet points, but they are **not** the presentation. Your slides should not repeat what you're saying.

## When should you use slides?

Slides are a tool to clarify your story, not only to impress your audience. Only use slides for things you can't explain briefly in words: diagrams, statistics, maps, and charts. Include one slide with an overview of the presentation and one slide with the conclusion. Avoid long lists, if you have to write something.

## Two resources on making slides

This book is not about making slides. Two books that do a great job explaining this are:

**Presentation Zen:** *Simple Ideas on Presentation Design and Delivery,* by Garr Reynolds

A slideshow should visually support what the speaker is presenting and not outline the speaker's points. This book clearly explains the notions of what an audience can or cannot grasp from a slideshow while someone is speaking and it gives a rich assortment of visual examples as well as links to rich online sources for images.

**Slide:ology:** *The Art and Science of Creating Great Presentations,* by Nancy Duarte

Her book goes into the science of audiences and presentations a bit more. Again, her book is richly illustrated with great examples.

## How many slides?

Use as few slides as possible. Edit slides out. Once you have reviewed your presentation, go through and cut slides out. Every creative process, from authoring books to movie making, involves an editing process where content gets cut. Force yourself to do this (it's hard at first because we don't want to drop anything we spent time creating!).

**When in doubt, leave it out! Ask yourself:**

- How does this help my audience understand my key message?

- Does it move us forward to the "happy ending"?

- How does it reinforce a soundbite or tagline?

## How to make a slide

Use fewer words and more images on your slides, even if it's a technical presentation. Beware of overpowering with graphics, special effects and sound. Remember that you're the expert, not the technology or software!

**Here are some basic tips for slide design:**

1. Use one font for titles, another for body text.

2. Smallest font you should use is a 36-point.

3. Avoid more than three or four lines of text at a time.

4. Use only the top 80% of the available space on the screen so even people at back of room can see.

## How long per slide?

Certain slides may require only a few seconds. Others may trigger a story. Spend no more than 2 minutes per slide. You can black out the screen using the B button when you are not using the slideshow.

# Use unique graphics instead of run-of-the-mill clipart

ClipArt.com has over 10 million download images available by subscription including photos, line drawing and clip art.

# Use these methods to practice short deliveries:

**Toastmasters.** Practice delivering your speech within 5 to 7 minutes without slides.

**Pecha Kucha.** If you use slides, try this method. Deliver your presentation using 20 slides and spend 20 seconds per slide. Set up your slideshow to autoplay every 20 seconds. You will soon realise that visual images are more powerful (and simpler) than words.

**Ignite.** What if you only had five minutes on stage to make your point? And what if you could use only 20 slides that automatically advanced every 15 seconds? Try this method to sharpen up your delivery until it's very tight. Remember that a 5 minute presentation can be reused and expanded. It's easy to go from 5 minutes to 10 minutes, not so easy the other way.

# Seven alternative presentation softwares

**Mindmanager**
www.mindjet.com

> *Tool for creating mind maps allowing a non linear approach to presentations. The presentation mode dynamically folds and unfolds parts of a complex mind map. This allows you to zoom into the details, while still keeping an eye on the context.*

## WHY USE PICTURES?

**A picture not only says a thousand words, it also increases retention.** We have an amazing memory for pictures. According to Dr. John Medina, visuals can push retention of a subject from 10% (spoken only) to 65% (spoken with visuals). When choosing a picture, ask:

*Does it add value to my presentation?*

*Does it reinforce a key message?*

*Is it appropriate?*

## FIND MORE PRESENTATIONS

YouTube is a great resource for videos. You can find presentation slideshows of all kinds. Check out Steve Job's product demonstrations (start with the iPod) and also the TED Talks presentations. They are awesome. You will find extremely broad and complex topics brought down to an engaging 15-20 minute presentation.

### Keynote available for Mac users

www.apple.com/iwork

> *Create absolutely stunning, cinema-quality presentations more easily than ever before.*

### Mindapp

www.mindapp.com

> *Another mind map software enabling brainstorming and creative thinking.*

### OpenOffice Impress

www.openoffice.org

> *Open Source version with similar features to PowerPoint.*

### Animoto

www.animoto.com

> *Helps create professional video with already licensed music.*

### Word processor

> *Use with large fonts and images on full screen mode.*

### Web browsers

> *Show web site using forward and back buttons.*

## How to work with a projector screen:

1. Do not face the screen. Look at your audience.

2. Set up a notebook in front of you or to the side so that you can keep track of the slides.

3. Use a wireless remote to move slides.

4. Press "B" to black out the screen in slideshow mode.

## Checklist:

- Be brief
- Be ready to present without any slides
- Do not read from the slides
- Few simple lines of text to illustrate your key point for that slide
- Limit text to 5 -7 words per line
- Make slides like a billboard: use simple attention grabbing pictures
- Use a visual to represent meaning
- Use music only to invoke a specific emotion from the audience
- Use only headlines & pictures. Speak the rest
- Summarize benefits for the audience attending the presentation
- Create no more than 20 slides

## HOW SIMPLE IS YOUR ENGLISH?

You don't need a large vocabulary to express yourself. Here are three systems using around 1000 words, much simpler than the 100,000 words in a medium sized dictionary.

1. Basic English devised in 1920s by Charles Ogden using only 850 words.
**ogden.basic-english.org**

2. Simplified Technical English derived by the aerospace industry with 900 word vocabulary.
**www.asd-ste100.org**

3. Voice of America Special English started in 1959 with 1,500 word vocabulary
**www.voanews.com/ specialenglish**

## USE OTHER TOOLS

### You need to become proficient with:

Flipcharts

Whiteboards

Live demonstrations

Role plays

## Tips for handouts:

1. Put all your complex information on handouts, such as data driven information and complex charts.

2. Distribute after your talk (not before or during) so people are focused on you and not reading through their handouts. You will lose eye contact and connection.

### Next chapter

Give enough presentations and you will be interrupted. Learn next about the Five Golden Rules and the four categories of the most frequently faced interferences. Let's "Manage all Interruptions".

# – 9 –

# Manage all Interruptions

"Circumstances may cause interruptions and delays, but never lose sight of your goal. Prepare yourself in every way you can."

*Mario Andretti, Italian born American race driver, b.1940.*

## This chapter's content:

### The 4 main areas of interruptions:

▶ A. Environment.
*Page 138*

▶ B. Movement.
*Page 140*

▶ C. Noise.
*Page 144*

▶ D. Malfunctions.
*Page 148*

## One Minute Learning:

● The Five Golden Rules of managing interruptions
*Page 137*

● Control the presentation room
*Page 138-139*

● Manage people and things moving around the place
*Page 140-143*

● Overcome external and internal distractions
*Page 144-147*

● Prepare for equipment failures
*Page 148-151*

## Process:

☞ First, read the five golden rules of managing interruptions.

☞ Second, skim the four main interruption areas.

☞ Third, look for specific solutions to frequent interruptions you face and prepare yourself even better for your next presentation.

## Case study#6:
## Enmo Noma, chairman, industrial services.

Enmo Noma was a dedicated presenter with years of carefully planned presentations to his partners, peers and superiors across Asia Pacific and North America. In many ways, he was a *One Minute Presenter*. He understood and could engage his audience with a message that was concise, clear and sometimes even humorous. However, if there was one gap in Mr Noma's presentation arsenal, it was whenever something unexpected happened during a presentation. Whenever a noise distracted the audience or they started talking among themselves or a mobile phone started buzzing, Mr Noma started to feel flustered (although he still looked calm on the outside). It threw him off his message and he tended to rush through the rest of his presentation. Once his computer could not connect to the projector and he was very embarrassed to stand in front of his waiting audience without his slides or video. Mr Noma had never prepared for the so-called unexpected.

This chapter makes you aware of most of the interruptions you will face in a presentation. It will also equip you with five golden rules to manage them, plus specifics tips to keep you on track.

## SMALL, MEDIUM AND LARGE ROOM SETTINGS

**Small room:**
a meeting room for audience size up to 20.

**Medium room:**
a special conference room on site, in a business center or hotel's meeting room. Audience size 20-50.

**Large room:**
a hotel ballroom or conference center held at an external venue. Audience size 50-500.

The Merriam Webster dictionary defines interruption as something that 'stops or hinders by breaking in'. In fact, if you take the word back to its Middle English root, the meaning is to plunder, or rob and tear away, which is exactly what an interruption can do to a presentation. All the hard work you have invested on treasuring your audience and producing your message to connect with your audience can be torn away by an interruption. Like Enmo Noma, if you cannot manage these interruptions then your effectiveness as a presenter will diminish in the eyes of your audience. Essentially a poorly managed interruption distracts the audience from the delivery of your message.

There are two stages to managing any interruption. The first is awareness, the second action. In the first stage of awareness, you become tuned into what can possibly interrupt a presentation. There are four main categories under which 99% of all interruptions can be placed. We'll look at them below. The second stage is the action stage. Prior to action you need to ask *"Should I do anything right now?"* This will depend on the intensity and frequency of the interruption, as well as the size of the audience and meeting room.

## Becoming more aware

You need to be aware and open to what is going on around you. Some of the interruptions in this chapter will be new to you and some may even sound far fetched. A *One Minute Presenter* is tuned into the interruptions going on, makes decisions on which ones need immediate attention and which ones can be left, and is always prepared and ready to react to malfunctioning equipment. This chapter will help you be ready for 99% of all interruptions.

## THE FIVE GOLDEN RULES OF INTERRUPTIONS:

1. Always keep your sense of humor
2. Be prepared for 99% of typical interruptions
3. Don't let your ego get the better of you
4. Be nice to the onsite support guys
5. If all else fails, see Rule #1

## How do interruptions interfere with effective communication?

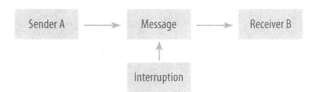

Most models of effective communication involve a sender (A) who is delivering a message to another person, the receiver (B) through a particular medium (like a presentation) and the degree to which this message does not get through is due to various interruptions.

Most interruptions come under four areas: environment, movement (of people and things), noise and malfunctions.

# A. Environment

Become familiar with all aspects of your presentation room:

## Layout

| Room Size: | All |
|---|---|
| **Interruption:** | Obstacles such as flipcharts, whiteboards and chairs block smooth movement around the stage. |
| *Actions you can take:* | Arrive early and work with venue staff or colleagues to make sure that your stage is clear and you have a unimpeded path to move comfortably from flip chart, laptop and around the audience. |

## Temperature

| Room Size: | All |
|---|---|
| **Interruption:** | **Scenario 1:** Outside it's a hot 35°C; inside icicles are forming on the ceiling. |
| | **Scenario 2:** Outside it's a hot 35°C; inside the heaters are turned on and eggs are frying themselves. |
| | **Scenario 3:** Outside it's a chilly -10°C; inside it's so cosy that people are curled up asleep glad of some warmth. |
| | **Scenario 4:** Outside it's a chilly -10°C; inside an iceberg has just floated down the hall. |
| *Actions you can take:* | You can control this 95% of the time. |
| | Work with the venue to ensure that the room's temperature will not distract from your presentation. An ideal temperature is 25° or 26°C. |

# Lighting

| Room Size: | All |
|---|---|
| **Interruption:** | The fluorescent lights are on so bright that people need to wear sunglasses and the slideshow is not visible on the screen. |
| *Actions you can take:* | Get familiar with the light switches (most rooms seem to have hundreds of them these days). |
| | Talk with the venue light team and practice light settings that you need for both regular presenting and computer/video viewing. For large venues, remember the lighting guy's name and prompt him, *"Bill, can we go to video light setting?"* It looks professional. Don't rely on telepathy to communicate with the lighting guy. Do your homework ahead of time. |

# Smell

| Room Size: | All |
|---|---|
| **Interruption:** | Occasionally you will find a strange odor in the room. Perhaps the building was just fumigated with cockroach powder (has happened to me!) at the weekend. Maybe the rugby team were in for a few drinks the night before. |
| *Actions you can take:* | If possible, open windows to get some fresh air in at the beginning of the day and after lunch if temperature allows. |
| | If the smell is too persistent, make a judgment call on how much it will distract from your presentation. Ask for a room change as a last resort, or carry some nice incense. |

# B. Movement

All kinds of people, mobile devices and things can be moved in and out of your presentation room. Be ready for them:

## Cleaners

| Room Size: | Medium, Large |
|---|---|
| Interruption: | Clearing tables, cleaning room, hovering carpet. |

## Hotel staff

| Room Size: | Medium, Large |
|---|---|
| Interruption: | Wandering around serving tea/drinks. |

## Event organisers

| Room Size: | Large |
|---|---|
| Interruption: | Rushing around aimlessly, walking up on stage. |
| *Actions you can take:* | We can cover these groups together. First, please remember that there is a world going on outside your presentation (I know that's hard to believe considering how much effort you put into preparing for it). And a part of that outside world is people doing their jobs. These hardworking people are doing their best and are not deliberately trying to sabotage your presentation. |
| | **Remember Golden Rule 1:** *Keep your sense of humor.* So when a worker walks across the stage with his top off smoking a cigarette, he (not usually she) is on his way to do something essential to keep the venue up and running. This is what I tell myself. Most of the time, a smile to the audience or a *"Hello"* to the guy will be enough to turn the tension into a laugh. Move on. That's all you need to do. Get to know the hotel staff managing your room and the event organizers. Be nice to them. Don't you know how much pressure they are under! |

Remember their names and communicate with them about how you would like the event to run. If they do wander into your presentation unexpectedly carrying a large set of bongo drums, crack a joke, smile at them and hold the door for them as they shuffle out apologizing. We all have an ego but please don't use it to feel big over hardworking people who are just trying to do their jobs.

**Remember Golden Rule 3:** *Don't let your ego get the better of you.*

# Participants

| | |
|---|---|
| **Room Size:** | All |
| **Interruption:** | Coming in and out of room. |
| | Getting called out by colleagues, coming in late after breaks. |
| | Head bobbing as the five course lunch kicks in around 2.30pm and people start to drift off asleep. |
| | Pulling out laptops despite ground rules not to use them. |
| *Actions you can take:* | If the coming and going gets too frequent. Take a quick break and talk to your participants and see if there is a reason. Perhaps there is an emergency going on. It won't always be within your control but it's good to find out the root cause. For medium and larger meetings this will not always be possible so just be ready to keep moving forward. |
| | Post up the ground rules for your meeting. One of them should be *"start and finish on time".* Don't wait for late comers. |
| | When presenting after lunch, be ready for audience sluggishness. Prepare an interactive exercise. Have a Q&A session or find another way to keep people engaged with your presentation (See Chapter 7 "Create your Connection" on ways to interact and engage with your audience). |

# Bosses

| | |
|---|---|
| **Room Size:** | Small |
| **Interruption:** | The manager who arrives late and then says, *"Sorry to be late. Can we please start over again? I don't want to miss anything."* |
| | Boss who jumps in while you're presenting and starts giving your presentation. |
| ***Actions you can take:*** | Here's a test of how much you really want to be a *One Minute Presenter*. If you're faced with a superior coming into a meeting late and asking you to start over or recap. Say this: |
| | *"Hi John, Here is the agenda or handout. We're on slide 10. You haven't missed anything vital, but I can catch up with you after the presentation or during the Q&A session. Would that be alright? Great. Let's move on."* |
| | Never, never, never go back and start over. This is the quickest way to deflate your credibility and sends a signal to your audience that timing is flexible and exceptions can always be made. This is not a good message to send out. |
| | When your boss jumps in to deliver some of your presentation, this could be because you have not run through your plans with your boss beforehand. Spend a couple of minutes, especially if it's a common or frequently delivered presentation like a company credentials, to check in with your boss and get his take on how you should approach the presentation. The audience is unique every time, so highlight areas that they may be more interested in. Ask your boss which areas to focus on and which ones to skip through lightly. This investment will help you both get settled with the presentation and prepare you both for how the presentation will go. Your boss may still chip in from time to time, but once he knows that you're in control he will likely sit back and watch you do your good stuff. |

# Things

| Room Size: | Medium, Large |
| --- | --- |
| Interruption: | Things that often get moved around hotel and conference spaces. And dropped. |
| *Actions you can take:* | You can't control this. Things are going to get dropped from time to time and they probably won't distract from your presentation that much.<br>**Golden rule 1: *Keep your sense of humor and think of a few punchlines.***<br>For example, this suggestion from motivational humorist, Scott Friedman:<br>*"...and that concludes the musical part of my program."* |

# Mobile devices

| Room Size: | All |
| --- | --- |
| Interruption: | Held firmly, looked at intently and then promptly dashed outside for another important call. |
| *Actions you can take:* | Nothing is going to prompt more movement in and out of your room than mobile devices.<br>If you have set your ground rules, then you can ask participants to step out if they have a call. Some people will take that to heart and be zipping in and out of the room all day. Ultimately, you can't control this unless they are your direct reports, so see if you can have a side conversation (not in front of everyone else) and ask him or her to moderate the call taking and keep them confined to the break times.<br>If you have a ground rule that laptops are not to be used (more difficult to enforce during an onsite presentation), then you can quietly ask the keyboard tapper to check his emails during the next break. That usually does the trick. I avoid calling people out and forcing them to back down in front of the group as it undermines their position and won't help you build a connection with them again in the future. **Remember Golden Rule 3: *Don't let your ego get the better of you.*** |

# C. Noise

Don't let noise from inside or outside your presentation room prevent you from getting your message across:

## Music

| Room Size: | Medium, Large |
|---|---|
| **Interruption:** | Loud external music from another conference room or from massive outdoor TV billboards located outside room window. |
| | Piped muzak inside room (sometimes on a centrally controlled timer). |
| *Actions you can take:* | Music blasting from the 500 seat ballroom next door, where a direct marketing company's most vibrant sales reps are celebrating their year end bash, can be distracting to say the least. You can request a new room and communicate assertively with the venue's staff or you can try to work around it. My best suggestion when working in external larger venues is to make this a question you ask the venue: |
| | *"What other events do you have in the venue at the same time as our presentation? Will they interfere with our presentation?"* |
| | Piped in muzak can usually be switched off. Maintain good relations with venue staff. Be polite and explain why the muzak might interfere with your presentation. |
| | Outside-the-venue distractions, such as the massive TV billboards pumping out nightclub music at 100 decibels, are becoming a part of city life. I found myself giving a presentation in Shanghai where we literally could not hear ourselves talk due to the outdoor intrusion. We went out and luckily the TV billboard had a telephone number of the advertising company. A couple of quick calls (helps to have a local person on hand if this happens to you outside your home country) and we had the volume turned down. Sometimes you just need to get out there and be proactive. |

# Air conditioner

| Room Size: | Medium, Large |
|---|---|
| Interruption: | Last serviced in 1987 and sounding the worse for wear. |
| *Actions you can take:* | Check the venue ahead of time. If the sound is unbearable, request a room change. Alternatively use a microphone even with a small group. In a total last resort, use electric fans instead if it's a small group. |

# Doors

| Room Size: | All |
|---|---|
| Interruption: | Slam shut and creak open (as participants come in and out). |
| *Actions you can take:* | Squeaky and slamming doors can become a distraction if people are frequently coming in and out. You can lock one door and force people to use another (less squeaky) one. You can also ask the venue staff to oil the hinges. It's a request they don't get every day. Say it with a smile and you will be surprised how easily it will be fixed. |

# Mobile phones

| Room Size: | All |
|---|---|
| Interruption: | Beeping or blasting polyphonic ring tones ("Titanic" or "Who let the dogs out"). |
| *Actions you can take:* | Ground rules should include a "mobile off" or an easier to enforce "mobiles to silent mode." Remember to switch off your own mobile. Nothing brings your credibility crashing faster than everyone hearing your "Backstreet Boys remix" polyphonic ringtone! |

# People

| Room Size: | All |
|---|---|
| Interruption: | Talking, side conversations or mini-debates often whispered. |
| | Snoring after a heavy lunch (Ouch). |
| *Actions you can take:* | People will talk and sometimes have side conversations. Your ground rules can include a "one conversation at a time" or a "one person speaks, we all listen" item. You need to make a judgment call. Occasional short conversations are inevitable. Longer, louder ones can be brought to a halt, by directing your presentation towards the people talking and giving them a smile. |
| | I recommend that you do *not* ask those people a question while they are talking. It's going to be obvious that they will not be able to answer you with confidence, leading to them losing face in public. You now have two people against you in the audience. Your ego may feel better, but you have taken a step away from your primary purpose of connecting with your audience and delivering a message with style. |
| | I hope it never happens to you, but if you're running longer workshops or presentations you may find people nodding off after a lunch. An hour at the buffet table can take its toll. In a large room setting, just ignore it. If you're faced by someone snoring in a room of 10, take a quick timeout or go to an interactive exercise. This hub of activity perks up the audience. Perhaps suggest a quick walk for some fresh air or a strong cup of tea or coffee. |
| | **Remember Golden Rule 1:** *Always keep a sense of humor.* |

# Construction

| Room Size: | All |
|---|---|
| Interruption: | Outdoor (and sometimes indoor) construction crashing and banging at high decibels. |
| *Actions you can take:* | This is a tough one. It's like the loud music above. Ask ahead of time. Scout out the venue early and see if you can secure another room if possible. |

# Fire alarm

| Room Size: | All |
|---|---|
| Interruption: | An important interruption that should be acted on immediately. |
| *Actions you can take:* | I recommend against continuing your presentation! Leave the building calmly. |

# D. Malfunctions

If a device works now, it could be broken in a minute. So be ready:

## Microphones

| Room Size: | Medium, Large |
|---|---|
| **Interruption:** | Silent spots on a stage. |
| *Actions you can take:* | Silent spots are spaces on the stage where the microphone goes dead. You can test this ahead of time and ensure that you don't step into these silent spots. |
| **Interruption:** | Batteries run out on handheld or clip-on microphones |
| *Actions you can take:* | Handheld microphones and clip on microphones (lavalier) can go dead suddenly. Make sure you know the sound guy by name and get his mobile phone if he is not based in the room. Be friendly with him during rehearsals. This humanity will pay itself back many times over when you're in a tight spot. The sound guy can pop up with batteries when you need them. Prepare two handheld microphones, which can be placed on the lectern. You can also have a fixed stand at the back or just off stage for back up. It's rare that all three would go down at the same time (given that you had tested them just before). |
| **Interruption:** | Feedback when the microphone comes too close to one of the big speakers. |
| *Actions you can take:* | Similar to silent spots, you need to check out the feedback areas, which give off a high pitched squeal (the sound from the speakers are picked up by your microphone, made much louder and put out as a loud squeal). Do your preparation with a thorough microphone test. Identify any area that needs to be avoided. Ask the sound guy. |
| | Always do sound checks as close to your presentation as possible so that configurations are set (and hopefully not changed any more). |

# Laptops

| | |
|---|---|
| **Room Size:** | All |
| **Interruption:** | Refuse to connect to the projector but worked fine in the rehearsal.<br><br>Power cable won't plug into extension sockets. |
| *Actions you can take:* | Test your laptop with the projector and once it works, keep it connected if at all possible. If you're part of a series of presentations, I would suggest you use the platform computer. Load up your presentation and test it on this computer with all your sound, slide deck and videos. If you have to use your own computer and connect it just before your presentation, make sure with the event planner that you have sufficient time to do that and bring the AV guy along with you to help connect it. This will ensure you're connected 99% of the time.<br><br>For the other 1% try doing the Mexican wave with your audience (it might be fun).<br><br>Extension cables are usually provided by the venue but there is no harm in bringing your own. Label it clearly so it doesn't walk away. It's a back up you may never use, but will bring you peace of mind. |

# Projectors

| | |
|---|---|
| **Room Size:** | All |
| **Interruption:** | Refuse to connect to the computer having worked fine during rehearsal. |
| *Actions you can take:* | Projectors and laptops today are more compatible so it's getting easier to plug and play modern computers with modern projectors. Occasionally after an operating system upgrade issues arise. Do your testing before the presentation. Be nice to the IT guy and once you have your connection, try to leave it connected. It will reduce your stress level, and avoid the risk of uncomfortable scrambling around in front of the audience (who are now reaching for their mobiles). |

# Electricity

| Room Size: | All |
|---|---|
| Interruption: | Are you ready for a black out? |
| *Actions you can take:* | Okay, this one could be a challenge. Even I'm not going to suggest you bring around a bundle of candles in your case (unless its someone's birthday). |
| | I do suggest that you charge up your laptops, digital video cameras and rechargeable batteries because sometimes you need to plug in a camera to show a video and you will find no socket available (unless you followed the tip above and have brought your own extension cable). |
| | If the electricity does cut out, gather everyone around the mobile phone screens and tell each other campfire stories. Now that would be an unforgettable experience! |

# Audio visual

| Room Size: | All |
|---|---|
| Interruption: | Music doesn't play. |
| | Videos won't play (nice big red cross on the screen). |
| | Slide show won't slide. |
| | All having worked perfectly in the rehearsals. |
| *Actions you can take:* | By now you should understand that testing ahead of time, befriending the tech guys and retesting as close to the presentation as you can will eliminate 99.9% of all the malfunctions you will come across. |
| | If an important video or song does not play, move on. The audience won't mind too much if you complete your presentation and deliver an engaging message. Okay the bells and whistles weren't there but what's more important: having |

the audience remember your message, or having them remember that you spent 10 minutes struggling to play a video, rebooting your computer and telling them how important and great this video was? Then, finally giving up and talking them through the video. I have seen it folks and it's not pretty.

Stay focused on creating the connection with the audience and delivering with style with or without technology.

## Next chapter

It's the part that presenters dread: the question and answer session. Let's introduce some tools to help you confidently "Master the Q&A".

# – 10 –

## THE SEVENTH STATION:

# Master the Q&A

"Chance favors the prepared mind."

*Louis Pasteur, French chemist and microbiologist, 1822–1895.*

## This chapter's content:

▶ A. Why does the Q&A fill us with fear?
*Page 156*

▶ B. How to prepare for the Q&A.
*Page 157*

▶ C. Running a Q&A session.
*Page 158*

▶ D. Following up a Q&A session.
*Page 165*

▶ E. Mastering difficult questions.
*Page 165*

## One Minute Learning:

● How to open a Q&A session
*Page 158*

● The 4As method for answering questions
*Page 158-161*

● Think quick with two way hooks
*Page 162-163*

● How to close your answers
*Page 164*

● Master difficult questions
*Page 165*

## *Process:*

☞ First, go and study the 4As method for answering questions. This gives you a structure for your next Q&A.

☞ Second, look through the 'think quick' example, which shows how you can shape an answer immediately.

☞ Third, skim through the rest of the chapter and find tips and suggestions to help you through this challenging session.

# Case study#7:
## *Ann, human resources director, professional services.*

Ann is very nervous about the Q&A. The feeling of not knowing what is coming next is sometimes overpowering. Ann hates it when she cannot think of an answer. It's too difficult to think of a competent reply so quickly. She always remembers the right answer after the presentation. Sometimes she is asked an unexpected question and that gives her a lot of pressure, especially when she is not sure about the best answer. Compared with her presentation, her answers are not as clear and logical as the rest of her presentation.

The pressure that Ann feels is very common for business presenters. Unless you were in the debating team at school, you probably have not been trained in how to overcome the pressure of not knowing what question is coming next and putting a competent answer together.

This chapter will help you prepare for your next Q&A session, manage the session, follow up where necessary and master those difficult questions.

# A. Why Does the Q&A Fill us with Fear?

H.P. Lovecraft, an American poet and author, referred to fear as mankind's "oldest and strongest" emotion. He identifies "fear of the unknown" as the deepest fear for both adults and children. It's no wonder that questions can fill us with nerves and tension!

### There are many ways to describe unprepared speaking:

- Speaking off the cuff
- Impromptu speaking
- Extemporaneous speaking
- Speaking on your feet

### Common situations requiring unprepared speaking:

- Q&A session during or after a presentation
- Unplanned telephone calls
- Boss walking up and asking a question
- Saying a few words at your annual dinner
- Speaking with media
- Joining a round table discussion

# B. How to Prepare for the Q&A

Despite the fact that unprepared speaking is an important part of life, most people shy away from this kind of speaking because of the lack of preparation time, the increased nerves and the panic of *"What am I going to say?"*

You **can** prepare for Q&A sessions. It's a myth that you can't. There are only a limited number of questions that you get asked. We'll now look at how to prepare and handle questions.

## Anticipate the questions

What will the audience ask you about? For example, if you're in sales or business development, you can prepare for the questions that your clients will ask you. There are a fixed number of areas including company background, your experience, product range and so on.

Fully 90% of these questions can be anticipated. There is rarely such thing as a unique question. Someone has asked it before. If you're not sure what questions you will be asked, do some research! Find people in your organization who have experience in this area and ask them what common questions you can expect.

**UNDERSTAND A SHORT AND SNAPPY APPROACH TO COMMUNICATING**

Life explained. On film. Experts, like Dr. Edward M. Hallowell, are interviewed with short 20 to 30 second replies on commonly asked questions.

*See www.videojug.com*

Sometimes you can leave content out of your presentation in order to lead the audience to ask a question about that area. This can help because you will then be ready for that type of question. If you're presenting on planning, then common areas would include the resources needed, budget, manpower, the impact for other areas of the business, how competitors will react and so on. You can think of some other areas. Write them down. Make your own Frequently Asked Questions (FAQ) list.

# C. Running a Q&A Session

Depending on your skills and attitude, questions can either unnerve and sidetrack or clarify and strengthen your presentation. Planning makes the difference. At the start of your Q&A session, briefly set "the rules." You can include:

- The length of the Q&A

- Ask that questions be related to your topic

- Limit one question per person

Once you have set the context, you can use the 4As method to manage the Q&A session.

## The 4As method

The 4As method is a simple technique that you can use to structure your answers. The 4As stand for: **attend, acknowledge, ask, answer.**

1. Attend to the question in full.

2. Acknowledge the questioner.

3. Ask to clarify and check

4. Answer the question.

## 1. Attend to the question in full

Listen to the entire question. Resist the urge to jump in before the question is finished. This premature interruption can lead to false assumptions and comes across as abrupt and disrespectful.

Beyond the specifics of the question, understand what is being asked. You may want to rephrase the question and ask, *"Did I understand you correctly?"* Correct factual errors or misunderstandings immediately.

Use your body language to make a connection with the questioner. Maintain steady eye contact. Lean towards the questioner. You can also tilt your head so that your ear is facing the questioner. This shows that you're listening carefully. Try to position your body so that you're facing them in an open stance. Stay focused on them the whole time. Avoid the temptation to look at your watch, or computer or play with your clicker. Nod your head or verbally agree as you comprehend the question. Relax and adopt a helpful attitude.

## 2. Acknowledge the questioner

Remember that the Q&A section is an opportunity for you to further your credentials as an expert in your field. It's not a contest of wills. It's not a battle of wits. It's not "you versus the questioner". Use the Q&A session to build even closer bonds between you and your audience. You should acknowledge every questioner. Make them feel good about asking a question, *"Thank you for your question. I appreciate the chance to address the issue you raise."* or *"That's a good observation, Bill. In fact, I was just discussing this with a client last week."*

After you have answered the question and checked that the questioner is happy with your answer, remember to go back and thank them again, by name, *"Thank you Bill.* (look around the room) *Is there another question?"*

### 3. Ask to clarify and check

Repeat the question only if necessary. If someone asks a question in a large audience without using a microphone or if your presentation is being taped, you should repeat the question. This helps all the audience hear the question, as well as giving you time to think about your answer. You can clarify the question with a checking question. So you can reply, *"So are you more interested in part A or part B?"* The questioner will tell you and then you can answer. The thinking here is that by asking a question you stay in control. In many environments (sales meetings, job interviews, police interrogation!), the person asking the questions stays in control.

Also, by asking a question you're confirming that you have understood the question and provided a choice to the questioner. It's a very interactive way to handle a question. Be careful not to overuse this particularly if you're checking very simple facts.

If you did not catch a word or phrase from the question, ask the questioner to repeat it. Or test that you understood their main point. You may rephrase the question and ask, *"Did I understand you correctly?"*

Challenge the question only if there are factual errors. Also, clarify any part of the question that may be misunderstood immediately. Confirm with the questioner that the restatement is acceptable, *"Rob, when you said the return on sales, did you mean for 2007 or year to date 2008?"* Or, *"John, thank you for your question. I would like to consider that from the marketing perspective. Would that be okay?"*

### 4. Answer the question

Once you have acknowledged the questioner and clarified the question, now talk to the audience, not just the questioner. You need to open out your answer to the whole audience for two reasons. Firstly, to keep them engaged and interested. If you only address one person, it starts to feel like a private conversation and the BlackBerry and mobile phones come out. Secondly, other people in the audience may have the same concerns, and by delivering to them as a whole, you're observing their reactions and noticing if you have covered their concerns. Look for the heads nodding in approval. If you start to see frowns, or a couple of people start side-talking, you may have raised another issue or not covered the answer satisfactorily well enough for them. Once you have completed your answer and acknowledged the first questioner, go back and ask if he/she has a follow up question. Never go off on a sidetrack during your answer. Handle one questioner at a time. One question at a time. When you finish, look to some other part of the room and ask, *"Who else has a question?"*

Now that you have a format you use in your Q&A session, you will still need to answer the questions. Your ability to think quick on your feet will be a great asset.

## Pause for quality answers

Often the difference between a good answer and a panicked reply comes down to allowing yourself a few seconds of thinking time. In this time, your supercomputer brain will seek out the relevant information. In pure processing power, the average brain can handle about 100 million MIPS (Million computer Instructions Per Second), which is still faster than the most expensive supercomputers today. But this is where most people let themselves down. Immediately, after hearing the question, they launch into a reply, without pausing to think. Confident presenters take the time to think.

# How can you think quick?

One way is to use two way thinking hooks. Their purpose is to help you answer the question quickly and with clarity. These are quick tools to organize your thoughts. When asked a question, if you're able to give a short concise answer immediately, you enhance your credentials. Two-way hooks can be opposites or used to compare/contrast. Examples:

- Past/now

- China/England

- Quality/cost

- Speed/accuracy

- Management/technical

- Systematic/creativity

## Use two-way thinking hooks

**When you're asked a question:**

1. First, think of a two-way hook to "hang" your content.

2. Now, for each hook think of a couple of points.

3. Come up with an opening.

4. Deliver the content.

5. Finally, use a closing technique.

So if the question was: *"What's your sales forecast for next year?"* Your answer can be constructed in this way:

## 1. Find your two-way hook.

Possibilities include: company's view/sales person's view or past performance/future possibilities. You can think of other hooks, too! For this example, I'll choose the first one: company's view/sales person's view.

## 2. Think of a couple of points for each hook.

*Company:* profitability, performance, meeting customer's needs, growth, competitors.

*Sales:* reaching quota, commission, bonuses, workload, work life balance.

## 3. Come up with an opening.

*"There're two ways to approach this question. From the company's perspective and from the sales perspective."*

## 4. Deliver the content.

Point 1 from the company's view...

Point 2 from the sales' view...

## 5. Finally, use a closing technique.

*"So today I have shown that it depends whose view you take before you can answer the question."* Or *"So in conclusion, you can see how we can build up different forecasts based on which perspective we take."*

## What if you do not know the answer to the question?

The golden rule is don't make things up and hope nobody notices. In today's internet connected world, people can very quickly check your facts. This happened at a conference I attended where a presenter answered a question using a statistic from an industry report. Within one minute, a hand went up to challenge the presenter for misquoting. This damages your credibility greatly.

If the question is beyond the scope of your knowledge, don't be afraid to say, *"I don't know."* You could bring in a colleague who may handle this area more competently. Ideally, in this situation you will have prepared your colleague for this possibility. Alternatively, you can make a commitment to find out and get back to the questioner within a specific time frame: *"Mary, that's a little beyond the scope of today's presentation. I can follow up with human resources and get an answer to you by tomorrow morning. Would that work for you? Thank you."*

## When should you not answer a question in full?

Postpone questions that require lengthy answers. Give a brief answer overviewing the main areas. Identify areas that can be discussed further, and offer to discuss it in more detail later: *"Bob, that's a whole new area of discussion. I'm happy to take this off line with you individually after the meeting. The three main areas that we need to address are (1), (2) and (3). Let's set up a time to talk about that. Can we meet afterwards? Great. Thanks."*

## How to close your answer

Once you have given your reply, do a quick check back with the questioner. This is often overlooked and I feel that it's a little rude if you don't do this. A quick, *"Does that make sense to you?"* or *"Are you happy with that answer?"* or *"Is there anything else you need to know?"* is important to close the question and move on to another question. Otherwise you may find the issue coming back later in the Q&A.

If somebody says, *"No. I'm not happy with that answer."* Then this is great. You have a chance to handle and clarify on the spot. Your ability to handle these type of situations will be directly related to your credibility in the eyes of your audience. When challenged, ask the person, *"Which part would you like me to clarify"* and focus in on his/her concern.

# D. Following up a Q&A Session

After answering the last question of your Q&A, end with a short summary of your message and main point. If you have not been able to answer any question completely and made commitments to get back to someone, make sure that you immediately make a note. You may need to meet people to exchange business cards after a presentation, so a quick note will be essential to remember what you need to do after the presentation. Always follow up when you say that you will.

# E. Mastering Difficult Questions

Let's consider three types of difficult questions you may come across and how to master them:

## MORE TIPS ON HOW TO HANDLE A Q&A:

– Avoid sarcasm, criticism, or arrogance

– Keep your sense of humor

– Answer the question directly without being abrupt

– Use your answers to reinforce your message

– Avoid talking in depth about a whole new subject

– Treat it as a learning experience

– Feedback is essential to understand your audience

## a. Mini-speech questions

**Problem:** a questioner launches into a mini-speech without getting to a question.

**Solution:** politely interrupt the person to ask them to ask their question. Say, *"Excuse me, John, do you have a question?"* Or *"Could you get to your question please, Alice?"* If you find that too confrontational, you may wait for the questioner to finish, then check the question, *"Thanks Roger. You had some interesting points there. Let me see if I understand your question. Your question is..."* After answering that question, remind the audience - in the interest of time - to ask direct questions.

Your credibility is still on the line during the Q&A, and your ability to manage people will either enhance or erode your credibility in the eyes of the audience.

## b. Multiple part questions

**Problem:** a questioner strings a number of questions together.

**Solution:** if you have already stated that each questioner is limited to one question (which you should have done at the start of the Q&A), you may ask the questioner to select the most pressing question. Remember the golden rule: one questioner at a time, one question at a time. In a smaller setting, where you're expected to handle multiple questions, you may say, *"Thank you for your questions. As I hear it, you have three questions. I would like to start with (1)..."*

Start with the question that is the easiest to handle and can be concisely answered. Then after your answer, check with the questioner: *"Does that answer your question?"* When you get the confirmation, move on. *"Thank you. Now I would like to address (2)..."*

Then move onto the next question. Continue until you have run through all the questions. You could also make a brief summary to tie all the answers together at the end.

With a large audience, check if anyone else has a question first. If not, go back to the questioner with several questions. You can also offer to meet with them after the meeting to field their question.

## c. Rude questions

**Problem:** very rarely, you will be asked a rude question that attacks you personally.

**Solution:** first, remain calm. Do not get defensive or angry. If you overreact, your audience will remember your reaction long after they have forgotten how rude the question was. Briefly address the question and move onto the next person, *"Thank you. I think we share a different point of view. As I have already stated my position on that matter, I'll move on with another question."*

With time and preparation you will find that you're always ready for the Q&A session and you will rarely be caught out by questions. In fact, you will start to enjoy and look forward to the Q&A session because that is where you really get to know and understand your audience's concerns!

### Next chapter

You're almost at the end of your journey as a *One Minute Presenter*. Take a tip from the experts and "Finish on Time".

# – 11 –

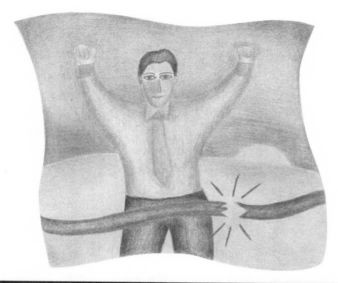

## THE EIGHTH STATION:

# Finish on Time

"Dost thou love life? Then do not squander time, for that is the stuff that life is made of."

*Benjamin Franklin, founding father, the United States of America, 1706–1790.*

## This chapter's content:

▶ A. Outlines.
   *Page 172*

▶ B. Timed rehearsals.
   *Page 172*

▶ C. Stay in control.
   *Page 177*

## One Minute Learning:

● Time tested formats to prepare for every presentation
   *Page 172*

● The key things to prepare thoroughly
   *Page 175*

● Adapt to last minute changes
   *Page 178*

## *Process:*

☞ First, refresh yourself on the outline of your presentation.

☞ Second, learn how to rehearse like a professional.

☞ Third, pick up a few tips on how to react to uncertainties and remain in control of your presentation's destiny.

# Case study#8:
## *Tim, technical director, mobile technology.*

Tim's working career bridged the research lab and client services. As an articulate and clear speaker on technical topics, he was often called upon to represent the company at conference and road shows to speak on the latest products and technology innovations. He enjoyed getting to meet a diverse group of people, although he did prefer one to one or small group meetings. Although he carefully prepared his presentations, he found it difficult to keep to his alloted time. Tim got excited about his topic and especially liked to talk about the technical nitty gritty details, which meant he took detours and side roads during his presentation.

One aspect of presentation that Tim did not like was when his time was cut right before he had to speak. *How could he just reduce this content by half? What did his boss expect him to do, speak twice as fast?* He often got visibly nervous at these times and this affected his delivery. He wondered whether his technique of rehearsing his presentation word for word was the best way to prepare given all the changes, which seem to be more frequent these days.

In this chapter, learn rehearsal techniques that will prepare you fully for every presentation, including those where the time gets cut down just before!

# A. Outlines

Good structure is the key to a good presentation. You can follow this time-tested flow that every good presentation uses:

| Speech Outline | Content |
|---|---|
| Opening | Make a Movie Message |
| Point 1 | Soundbite |
| Point 2 | Soundbite |
| Point 3 | Soundbite |
| Close | Happy Ending |

In the next section, we'll show how you can build up the content of your presentation from an outline to final delivery through systematic timed rehearsals.

# B. Timed Rehearsals

To look at how important rehearsals and practice are to perfecting your craft, let's hear from three legends from very different fields and generations:

*"Practice does not make perfect. Only perfect practice makes perfect."*
Vince Lombardi, American football coach.

*"I can never stop working hard. Each day I feel that I have to improve. Hard work...determination...I gotta keep pushing myself."*
Michael Jordan, basketball player.

*"I've always tried to find ways to give him adversity in practice and have him overcome it. The higher the level of pressure the better Michael performs. As expectations rise he becomes more relaxed...that's what makes him the greatest."*

Bob Bowman, coach to swimmer Michael Phelps.

## Rehearsing or making slides?

Does this sound like you before a big presentation? You want to prepare well in advance, so you spend hours and hours in front of your computer making your slides. When the day comes around, you still feel nervous. Although you got through the presentation, you felt that you could have been a lot more convincing. Why did all the preparation not produce better results? People spend too much time preparing their PowerPoint slides and elaborate charts and forget to spend any time rehearsing, which is crazy!

Can you imagine a theater group who spent all their rehearsal time modifying and refining their scripts and not spending any time on practicing how the script will look on stage? Never!

## Block time to practice

You should be spending a lot more time on rehearsing. Most people spend 90% of their time thinking about their content. Reduce this to 50% and spend 50% on rehearsal. For an important presentation which you have never given before, a rule of thumb is one hour of preparation and rehearsal for one minute of final delivery. So a 20-minute presentation needs 20 hours to get ready the first time you deliver it.

Your presentation is a good chance for you to play to your strengths (enthusiasm, interaction with the audience, engaging stories). Practice, practice, practice until you know your content cold. That is your starting point for excellence. Practice takes time. Book time into your calendar to rehearse. Make it a "to do" item. Start talking out your presentation as early as possible. This helps solidify ideas. Don't consider yourself fully prepared unless you have had 10-15 run throughs. We'll show you how to develop your material through rehearsals later in the chapter.

## Create space to practice

Practice needs space. Find a room or space where you will not be disturbed. You need to rehearse by speaking your presentation out aloud. I have rehearsed in my car, in the park and after hours in my office. Once you know your content, start to think about adding gestures. Start off by looking in a mirror (a full body one) and seeing how certain gestures can add impact on key phrases and words.

## Get feedback

**Follow this flow: paper to mp3 to video to 3rd party review.**

1. Start preparing your content on paper until you have an outline of ideas with some key sections.

2. Talk these ideas out aloud and note down the points that make sense to you or sound good. Practice this several times.

3. Record your presentation on your audio recorder or MP3. Break it

into sections and deliver the presentation as though you had an audience in front of you. Stand up while you deliver and imagine an audience or look in a mirror.

4. Write down the time it takes you to deliver each section. This will be important when it comes to finding areas to cut if time is short.

5. Finally, you may like to use a video recorder to capture your final rehearsals and see how you look while delivering. Note places where you can use gestures and body language to reinforce your messages.

6. After you feel good with your delivery, start to ask for feedback from your peers. Do a test run with your colleagues or even your family members. A friend of mine gives practice presentations to his wife and daughter. This is all valuable rehearsal time and will build up your confidence.

## Signpost your speech

Add in "time marks" after each major point so that you can keep an eye on your progress. For example:

| Section | Time Mark |
|---------|-----------|
| Opening | – |
| Point 1 | 7 minutes |
| Point 2 | 16 minutes |
| Point 3 | 23 minutes |
| Q&A | 27 minutes |
| Close | 30 minutes |

### Eyes.

Do you know what you look like when you speak in public? If not, you can start by looking in the mirror to get a feel for your body language and gestures. Watch out for repetitive gestures that are not adding impact. Also, watch out for bad habits like touching your nose, face or hair. If you have a video recorder, use it to review your presentations. It's hard at first but self awareness is an essential step on the road to more confident speaking.

### Ears.

Record your speech on a tape recorder or digital recorder. Record yourself on mp3 or video. Listen to yourself presenting. How convincing do you sound? Present as though the audience was in the room. Run through the presentation as though it was the real thing!

Write it as an accumulated time (not the timing for the individual sections). When you start your presentation you can quickly write down times you need to start each sections:

| 1500 | Start presentation. I go into my opening and first point. |
| 1507 | Start point 2. |
| 1516 | Start point 3. |
| 1523 | Start Q&A. |
| 1527 | Start close. |
| 1530 | Finish presentation and sit down. |

This is a handy guide to keep you on time as you move through the presentation.

## 20 rehearsals for a new speech or presentation

Use rehearsals 1 –7 to work your content into a **final draft**. Review Chapter 5 "Treasure Your Audience" and Chapter 6 "Produce Your Message."

Use rehearsals 8-11 to match your **vocal variety** with your content. See Chapter 8 "Deliver With Style."

Use rehearsals 12-14 to add **gestures** to your key messages. Refresh with Chapter 8 "Deliver With Style."

Use rehearsals 15-17 to add **questions** and increase interaction with your audience. See Chapter 7 "Create Your Connection" and Chapter 10 "Master the Q&A."

Use rehearsals 18-20 to **polish delivery**, check your timings and make sure you memorize your opening and closing sentences.

# C. Stay in Control

Have you ever been told you have 40 minutes to present and right before it's your turn, the meeting host asks you to present in 20 minutes! That means you have to cut serious corners, sometimes eliminate entire sections to fit the time. How can we do this without losing our main messages? We need to be ready for this so we can stay in control.

## Bullet train or steam train

Your presentation is like a train journey. You have a final destination (your happy ending) with stops (stations) along the way. If you have time you can stop off at a station and explore the local surroundings, check out a nice coffee and cake shop or visit a local museum and meet local people. If you have a lot of time, you can do that at every station. But say you suddenly got a call from the office asking you back to the office tomorrow, *what would you do?* Well you can still take the next train and travel straight through to your final destination. You stay in control of your journey and arrive at the same place. Finishing on time is much like a train journey. Often the amount of time you planned and rehearsed is cut down at the last moment due to:

300 (2006), a great male bonding movie about 300 Spartans at the battle of Thermopylae in around 480 AD. There are 1,523 cuts in the film, with over 1,300 visual effect shots comprising 8,631 visual effect elements. This works out to one cut every 3 seconds.

This is typical of most action movies today and the quick changes attune our brains, so that we are now finding it much harder than before to see and focus on one thing for a long time. When presenting you need to factor in your own "cuts"- something that will grab the attention. For example, a personal story, or a video. Give a quick self-test to the audience. Or ask the audience to talk with their partner. The audience expects "cuts" and you have to deliver.

- Speakers in front of you using too much time

- Important client is leaving sooner than expected

- Boss asks you

## How to edit down

Whatever the reason, it's difficult to go from 40 minutes to 20 minutes immediately. It can be done, however. First, use the outlines above and write them down and carry them with you so that you have the framework for your presentation. Regardless of time, your opening and closing will not change much.

So you need to cut the time from your main points. Like on the train journey, you don't have to get off and spend lots of time in one place. For a main point, you can deliver the bare bones (the essential points) and then ask the audience to contact you afterwards if they would like more information. This often happens in technical presentations when you cut out large amounts of heavy data-based material (thank you for doing that by the way). This can lead to people coming up to you after the presentation and asking for more information. In a large conference setting this can be great because it filters out the people who are not interested and brings you closer to your targeted prospect. Maybe we should all deliver shorter presentations. How great would that be!

If you're not sure what to cut out here's a few tips:

| | |
|---|---|
| **Data-heavy information** | Charts, testing results, technical formulas which are usually packed onto PowerPoint slides.<br><br>**Action:** Provide on a handout or ask people to contact you after the presentation. |
| **Information about you** | Detailed slides on company history, great detail about your founders' early days.<br><br>**Action:** Give essential points that build your credibility and get back to being audience focused. |
| **Long rambling stories** | "Pet stories"of the presenter told over and over regardless of how well they connect to the presentation being delivered.<br><br>**Action:** Keep stories and anecdotes tightly linked to your key message with punchy snappy nuggets of 2 to 3 minutes. |
| **Unorganised slides** | Information is 'thrown' onto slides in no particular order or design.<br><br>**Action:** Find ways to group, name and organize your data details. Even for technical presentations, challenge yourself to make it more engaging and structured. |
| **Your inner voice** | Open with telling how nervous you are, how unprepared you are, or how you have never given a presentation on this topic before.<br><br>**Action:** Cut out the self doubting, and please don't share it in public. It's really painful (and tedious) to listen to. |

As you have practiced timed rehearsals above, you should be very familiar with your "sound bites" by now. You can use them to build up from the bare bones of your outline. Use a time tested formula that is engaging and gets your message across in the shortest possible time. This formula is used by the best business communicators around the world today. It's simple to remember. Here it is:

*"Make a point. Tell a story."*

*"Make a point. Give an example that shows it."*

Use this technique the next time your time is cut and you will still be able to deliver a compelling presentation.

## Next chapter

You did it! You've been through the 8 stations on the road to becoming a *One Minute Presenter*. But I know what you're thinking, so, what now? Let's run through a few simple steps you can take to get even more value from *The One Minute Presenter*.

# Part III

# – 12 –

## Call to Action:

# So What Now?

"You become a *One Minute Presenter,* one presentation at a time."

*Warwick John Fahy, author, The One Minute Presenter*

## This chapter's content:

▶ A. Buy extra copies and give them to people who present.
*Page 185*

▶ B. Visit the resources section.
*Page 186*

▶ C. Try something new every presentation.
*Page 186*

## One Minute Learning:

● More help is available
*Page 185*

● Go deeper with the expert resources
*Page 186*

● Learning starts with action
*Page 186*

## *Process:*

☞ First, look for alternative learning methods available from *The One Minute Presenter* team.

☞ Second, visit the Resources section to gain access to the best wisdom available on business presenting.

☞ Third, start using the tips found in this book. Every presentation put a tip to the test.

# A. Buy Extra Copies and Give Them to People Who Present

I may be accused of some shameless self-promotion, but it works for Steve Jobs who talks up Apple products at every opportunity, and he is a great role model for presenters everywhere.

I'm also an advocate for increasing awareness in better communication skills and decreasing the suffering that millions of people go through every day in the form of terrible presentations.

If you have a large team or would like to give this book as a gift, contact us for our quantity discounts and custom cover designs.

Feel free to quote me, excerpt or paraphrase me to get these important time saving messages out. Invite me to speak at your organization. See our web site at **www.oneminutepresenter.com** for how to arrange that.

We also offer other learning methods for small groups:

- Workshops
- Coaching
- Workbooks
- Self learning courses

Do you need more support for your training and HR teams. We have Train-the-Trainer (TTT) programs and workbooks.

**BUY ONE, GIVE ONE FREE.**

The more books we sell, the more books we can provide to under-financed schools and orphanages in Asia.

*See page 211 to learn more about how we share the joy of giving.*

# B. Visit the Resources Section

I have included some of the major influences on my thinking and also experts in the field of communication. Read their books. Visit their web sites. Learn from the best.

# C. Try Something New Every Presentation

Use this book as a reference guide that you can keep on hand while you're preparing for your presentations. Try out a new tip every time to deliver. Variety is the spice of life and even if you're delivering your company credentials presentation three times a week. Make each one special and unique. Every audience is unique. They deserve something special.

### Next chapter

For further reading, check out our resources section. There are loads of great reads and web sites to visit to further improve your skills.

We keep an up-to-date resources section at

**www.oneminutepresenter.com/resources**

# Resources

I have not attempted to cite in the text all the authorities and sources consulted in the preparation of this book. To do so would require more space than is available. The list would include departments of various governments, libraries, industrial institutions, periodicals and many individuals. We update our resources section. Check out **www.oneminutepresenter.com/resources** for new tools, tips and resources.

## Expert communicators

Darren LaCroix, 2001 World Champion of Public Speaking.
www.Humor411.com

Scott Friedman, author, *Using Humor For A Change* and *Punchlines, Pitfalls and Powerful Programs.*
www.funnyscott.com

Michael Michalko, author, *Thinkertoys (A Handbook of Creative Thinking Techniques), Cracking Creativity (Thinking Strategies of Creative Geniuses)*, and *Thinkpak*, a tool for brainstorming.
www.creativethinking.net

Harry E. Chambers, author, *My Way or the Highway: The Micromanagement Survival Guide* and *Effective Communication Skills for Scientific and Technical Professionals.*
www.harrychambers.com

Suzanne Bates, president and CEO Bates Communications Inc., author, *Speak Like a CEO* and *Motivate Like a CEO.*
www.bates-communications.com

Jim Key, 2003 World Champion of Public Speaking.
www.jimkey.com

W Mitchell, inspirational motivational speaker for overcoming adversity 2008–2009 President of the International Federation of Professional Speakers.
www.wmitchell.com

Bob Urichuck, international professional speaker, trainer and author, *Discipline for Life*, *You Are the Author of Your Future* and *Up Your Bottom Line*, Featuring the ABC, 123 Sales Results System.
www.BobU.com

Rodney Marks, comic presentations at business events.
comedian.com.au

Robyn Pearce, the Time Queen, Certified Speaking Professional, Past President, IFFPS (International Federation for Professional Speakers)
www.gettingagrip.com

Dan Poynter, the self-publishing guru.
www.parapublishing.com

Raleigh R. Pinskey, The Raleigh Group Communications, author, *101 Ways To Promote Yourself*, *The 8-Second Media Pitch*, and *Branding Basics*.
www.promoteyourself.com

## Chapter 1: Nobody is Listening

Marshall McLuhan, author, *Medium is the Message*.
www.marshallmcluhan.com

Dr. John Medina, author, *Brain Rules*.
www.johnmedina.com

Marc Prensky, originator of term "digital native".
*On the Horizon* (MCB University Press Vol 9 No5 October 2001)
www.marcprensky.com

A digital native research project.
www.youtube.com/berkmancenter

Dr. Edward "Ned" Hallowell, author, *Crazy Busy*.
www.drhallowell.com

Twitter, social networking and microblogging service.
www.twitter.com

Wikipedia, online multilingual free-content encyclopedia.
www.wikipedia.org

Myspace, social networking website.
www.myspace.com

Facebook, social networking website.
www.facebook.com

YouTube, video sharing website.
www.youtube.com

Attention Deficit Disorder Assocation.
www.add.org

## Chapter 2: Help is Here

Jack Stack, author, *The Great Game of Business*.
www.greatgame.com

Hans Rosling, creator, *Gapminder*.
www.gapminder.org

Ian Jukes and Anita Dosaj, researchers, digital natives.
web.mac.com/iajukes/thecommittedsardine/About_Us.html

Lord Saatchi, co-founder, advertising agency M&C Saatchi.
www.mcsaatchi.com

C and T, theater company using new technology to educate.
www.candt.org

TED, annual conference on technology entertainment design.
www.ted.com

SIFE, students in free enterprise, annual international contest.
www.sife.org

PSA China, professional speakers assocation.
www.chinaspeakers.org

Chopschticks, comedy show held across Greater China.
www.chopschticks.com

## Chapter 3: Your Roadmap

Earl Nightingale, pioneering motivational speaker.
www.earlnightingale.com

## Chapter 4: You, the Presenter

Eleanor Roosevelt, first lady, the United States.
www.feri.org

Walter Cannon, coined the term fight or flight.
www.the-aps.org/about/pres/introwbc.htm

Little Albert experiment, evidence of human conditioning.
www.sussex.ac.uk/psychology/documents/harris_-1979.pdf

Tiger Woods' golf mental secret revealed.
www.pressrelease365.com/pr/sports/golf/tiger-woods-golf-mental-secret-2044.htm

Toastmasters International, public speaking, leadership skills.
www.toastmasters.org

IFFPS, international professional speaking assocations.
www.iffps.org

## Chapter 5: Treasure your Audience

Mahatma Gandhi, Indian philosopher.
www.mkgandhi.org

World's oldest known portrait is 27,000 years old in a cave.
www.guardian.co.uk/artanddesign/2006/jun/06/art

Chris Garrett, professional blogger, articles on avatars.
www.chrisg.com

Lovemarks, philosophy of a future beyond brands.
www.lovemarks.com

## Chapter 6: Produce your Message

Plato, Ancient Greek philosopher.
plato.stanford.edu/entries/plato

Dr. Stephen Covey, author, *The 7 Habits of Highly Effective People.*
www.stephencovey.com

*Aliens*, scary space movie.
www.imdb.com/title/tt0078748

*Jaws*, scary shark movie, one of the first high concept films.
www.jaws30.com

Steven Spielberg, influential movie director.
www.imdb.com/name/nm0000229

*BusinessWeek*, business magazine published by McGraw-Hill.
www.businessweek.com

Google's open source browser Chrome.
www.google.com/chrome

*Aesop's Fables*, brief storries providing moral education.
www.aesopfables.com

*Harvard Business Review*, a monthly research-based magazine written for business practitioners.
www.hbr.org

Stanley Ralph Ross, writer of 1960s cult classics, like Batman.
www.imdb.com/name/nm0743853

## Chapter 7: Create your Connection

John Keller, creator, ARCS Model of Motivational Design.
www.arcsmodel.com

Robert Cialdini, social psychologist and author, *Influence*.
www.influenceatwork.com

Joe Girard, tagged as *"world's greatest salesman."*
www.joegirard.com

Aristotle, influential Greek philosopher.
ancienthistory.about.com/cs/people/p/aristotle.htm

Tony Robbins, peak performance coach.
www.tonyrobbins.com

Three of the best stand up comedians ever:
Bill Hicks, www.billhicks.com.
George Carlin, www.georgecarlin.com.
Richard Pryor, www.richardpryor.com.

Videos on how to use the techniques in this book.
www.youtube.com/oneminutepresenter

## Chapter 8: Deliver with Style

Zig Ziglar, legendary motivational speaker.
www.zigziglar.com

Two pastors with influential oratory:
Joel Osteen, www.joelosteen.com.
Rick Warren,www.rickwarren.com.

Dr. Chris Smith, making science accessible for all.
www.thenakedscientists.com

Cnet, reviews, news and prices on tech products.
www.cnet.com

Michael Phelps, winner of the most Olypmic gold medals.
www.michaelphelps.com

Red Bull, energy drink.
www.redbull.com

Edward Hall, author, *The Silent Language*.
en.wikipedia.org/wiki/Edward_T._Hall

Grand Canyon Railway, travel in style on vintage trains.
www.thetrain.com

Raleigh Pinskey, author, *101 Ways to Promote yourself.*
www.promoteyourself.com

Dr. Candice M. Coleman, author, *Say It Well!*
www.SayItWell.com

Desmond Morris, author, *PeopleWatching.*
www.desmond-morris.com

Alexander Technique, methods to improve posture.
www.alexandertechnique.com

Garr Reynolds, author, *Presentation Zen: Simple Ideas on
Presentation Design and Delivery.*
www.presentationzen.com

Nancy Duarte, author, *Slide:ology : The Art and Science of
Creating Great Presentations.*
www.slideology.com

Pecha Kucha, join a night of snappy presentations.
www.pecha-kucha.org

Ignite, events featuring 5 minute presentations.
ignite.oreilly.com

Rukmini Bhaya Nair, IIT professor traces Darwin's steps.
timesofindia.indiatimes.com/articleshow/223286.cms

The non verbal library.
www.linguaggiodelcorpo.it/biblio

Non verbal behaviour skills.
http://www3.usal.es/~nonverbal/introduction.htm

Chinese emotion and gesture.
http://www.ling.gu.se/~biljana/gestures2.html

## Chapter 9: Manage all Interruptions

Mario Andretti, Italian born American race driver.
www.marioandretti.com

## Chapter 10: Master the Q&A

Louis Pasteur, French chemist and microbiologist.
www.pasteurfoundation.org

H.P. Lovecraft, author, horror, fantasy, and science fiction.
www.hplovecraft.com

*The Great Debaters*, debate team takes on all comers.
www.thegreatdebatersmovie.com
Videojug, library of free factual video content online.
www.videojug.com

## Chapter 11: Finish on Time

Benjamin Franklin, founding father, United States.
en.wikipedia.org/wiki/Benjamin_Franklin

Three sports legends:
Vince Lombardi, American football coach.
www.vincelombardi.com

Michael Jordan, basketball player.
www.nba.com/playerfile/michael_jordan

Bob Bowman, coach to swimmer Michael Phelps.
en.wikipedia.org/wiki/Bob_Bowman_(coach)

300, a force of 300 men fight the Persians in 480 B.C.
www.imdb.com/title/tt0416449

# Acknowledgments

Scores of people influenced and contributed to this book. Many heart-felt thanks to:

*To my family:* Grandad, Mum, Wessley, Raphael, Liz.

*To my wife:* Rebecca.

*To my friends in Toastmasters:* Samuel Jones, Johnny Uy, Keith Ostergard, Darren La Croix, Victor Yu, Andy Guo, Yingdan Liu, Cher Tse, Maggie Shi, Corona Li, Tina Ma, Vivien Chen, Dawn Lin, Jorie Wu, George Yen, Darren Paproski, Bo Bennett, K Beate Richter, Friedhelm Maur, Michelle Li, Alice Xie, Cao Jie, Joy Wang, Sam Ng, Paul Miller (gone but not forgotten), Shanghai People's Square, Dynamic Mandarin, Talent Discovery and all the Toastmasters in China and around the world whom I have had the good fortune to meet during the past 8 years!

*To my XL friends:* Roger Hamilton, Dave Rogers, Mike Handcock, Paul Dunn, Tim Hansen, Frances Cheung, Masami Sato, Shanghai life members and all the inspiring social entrepreneurs who are taking action to change the face of business.

*To my professional speaking friends:* Raleigh Rudy Pinskey, Dan Poynter, Scott Friedman, Bob Urichuck, Robyn Pearce, Terry Brock, Roger Harrop, Donald Jessep, Rob Salisbury, David Berman, John Bell, Paul Bridle, Reg Athwal, Erik Barnes, Glenn Wilkinson, CJ Ng, Matthew "Rapping Professor" Bloomfield, Mark Millar, Michael Rosenthal.

*To the "Dr." dudes:* Dr. Desmond Morris, Dr. John Medina, Dr. Chris Smith, Dr. Edward M Hallowell, Dr. Alan Hirsch.

*To my teachers:* Zig Ziglar, Robert Kiyosaki, Wallace D. Wattles, Jack Stack, Eckhart Tolle, Benedictine Nuns of Nile Lodge, Napoleon Hill, Steven Covey, Brian Tracy.

*My team:* Kathrin Zimmermann, Charlene Vormeng, John Eggen, Lorna McLeod, Tom Robinson, Marini Widowati.

# Index

# A

# B

Dr. Chris Smith, 97, 194, 199

Dr. Desmond Morris, 112, 117, 124, 199

Dr. Edward M. Hallowell, 8, 157

Dr. John Medina, 5, 8, 9, 71, 130, 189, 199

Dr. Stephen Covey, 58, 192

## E

emphasis, 94, 99, 100, 104, 107, 108, 109, 117

engage, x, 9, 12, 13, 14, 29, 37, 64, 81, 85, 86, 87, 91, 113, 121, 135, 141, 160
    with audience, 85–87

enthusiasm, 37, 74, 86, 106, 107, 108, 174

environment, 6, 39, 44, 77, 85, 97, 103, 113, 134, 137, 138, 160

equipment failures, 134

expectations, 28, 40, 42, 43, 44, 45, 52, 60, 173

eye contact, 29, 76, 81, 90, 94, 112, 113, 114, 132, 159

## F

face, xi, 25, 33, 44, 94, 102, 112, 118, 123, 124, 146, 176

Facebook, 7, 68, 190

fear, 22, 25, 26, 31, 32, 33, 34, 39, 112, 118, 154, 156

fearbuster, 26, 34, 35, 38, 39, 40

feedback, 57, 65, 84, 148, 165, 174, 175, 213

flip charts, 74, 78, 83

## G

gestures, 89, 94, 98, 112, 116, 117, 118, 119, 120, 122, 174, 175, 176, 177 golden avatar, 42, 46, 47

ground rules, 74, 77, 141, 143, 145, 146

# H

hands, 2, 27, 32, 33, 59, 60, 78, 80, 115, 118, 121

Hans Rosling, 13, 190

happy ending, 54, 56, 58, 59, 61, 62, 66, 69, 70, 128, 172, 177

head, 37, 59, 60, 65, 80, 82, 97, 116, 141, 159, 161

heart, 16, 27, 31, 32, 33, 37, 59, 60, 65, 80, 143, 213

high concept, 56, 62, 63, 193

higher performing team, 213

hold attention, 74, 76, 79, 81

Hollywood, 54, 62, 65

hospitable space, 74, 83

humor, 76, 78, 87, 88, 137, 140, 143, 146, 165, 188

# I

Ian Jukes and Anita Dosaj, 15, 190

ignite, 129, 195

industrial services, 21, 135

information overload, 2, 7, 13, 69

interact, 15, 72, 74, 81, 84, 85

interruptions, xi, 19, 29, 64, 77, 81, 105, 133, 134, 135, 136, 137, 138, 139, 140, 141, 142, 143, 144, 145, 146, 147, 148, 149, 150, 159, 196

    manage all, 133–150

movie message, 54, 61, 62, 64, 66, 172

multitasking, 2, 4, 6, 8, 13, 76

# N

noise, 134, 135, 137, 144

non-verbal, 88, 89, 94, 112, 122, 123, 196

# P

pause, 94, 99, 100, 105, 110, 111, 161

Pecha Kucha, 129, 195

pitch or tone, 94, 99, 106

portrait, 40, 42, 44, 45, 46, 53, 192

postures, 94, 112, 115, 116, 195

presenter,

evaluate yourself as a, 28–29

professional services, x, 21, 155

Professional Speakers Association of China, xiii, 15

psychographics, 42, 44, 45

# Q

Q&A session, 29, 142, 154, 155, 156, 157, 158, 159, 161, 165, 167

questions, 33, 42, 45, 46, 48, 49, 50, 74, 75, 76, 78, 80, 82, 83, 84, 86, 122, 154, 155, 156, 157, 158, 160, 161, 164, 165, 166, 167, 177

build rapport with, 74–78

mastering difficult, 165–167

preparing for, 154–161

structure to answer, 158–161

## R

## S

## T

# Share the Joy of Giving

*"If we don't change we don't grow.
If we don't grow ,we aren't really living."*

Gail Sheehy

**Unique Voices Publishing** is a social enterprise and has committed to donate 10% of all revenue generated by the sale of this book to *The Library Project.*

Certified Social Enterprise
www.worldwidewealth.org

Giving is a strong part of our values. We support local community projects to help educate children so they have the opportunity to share their unique talents with the world.

Just by buying this book, a child gets that chance. Every time you buy a copy of *The One Minute Presenter*, a book is purchased automatically for The Library Project – a charity that provides books to under-financed schools and orphanages in Asia. Learn more about this worthy cause at **www.library-project.org**

Unique Voices Publishing are a member of Buy1GIVE1, a system that shares the joy of giving by bringing together business, charities and the customer in a way that has not been done before. See **www.buy1-give1free.com** to learn more.

# Ready to become a better presenter?

## Why work with a one-to-one communication coach?

Many executives who work with a communication coach have experienced career advancement and success in their positions because they can communicate more effectively. Top presenters, like Steve Jobs, use coaching to polish their performances. A coach targets obstacles, suggests techniques to overcome them and supports you through change with evaluation, encouragement and experience.

Our coaching programs are tailored exactly for you at a time to suit you. We work with senior executives and managers across Asia and the Middle East in three, six and twelve month development plans. Coaching is supported by audio feedback, video "instant replays" and weekly e-letters bringing you practical tips. For a *free* initial consultation (value 200 Euros) please email: **coaching@oneminutepresenter.com**

## Boost your bottom line with a higher performing team.

Poor personal communication is at the heart of most people problems. Overcome this by improving the presentation skills of your managers and customer facing teams. We have taken the time-tested techniques and tips from *The One Minute Presenter* and skillfully packaged them into a two day interactive hands-on workshop which can be delivered both in-house or off-site. Thousands of people have benefited with increased presenting confidence, improved on-the-job productivity and boosted business results. Companies with good communication skills have higher morale and retention. For a workshop package and free initial consultatation (value 200 Euros) please email: **workshops@oneminutepresenter.com.** Information about the book, as well as *The One Minute Presenter* retreats, seminars and executive boot camps, is available at **www.oneminutepresenter.com**

Breinigsville, PA USA
14 April 2011
259781BV00001B/64/P